This book was translated and compiled from the lectures of Shaykh-ul-Islam Dr. Muhammad Tahir-ul-Qadri, titled 'The Coming of Imam Mahdi' in the Urdu language.

Clarity Amidst Confusion:
Imam Mahdi & The End of Time

Translated from the lectures of
Shaykh-ul-Islam Dr. Muhammad Tahir-ul-Qadri

Minhaj-ul-Quran International
292-296 Romford Road
Forest Gate
London E7 9HD
United Kingdom

Visit us on the World Wide Web at:
www.minhajuk.org

First Published January 2008

Published by Minhaj-ul-Quran International (UK)

ISBN 095518883-0

Cover Design & Typeset by Uwais Muhammad Afzal & Tahseen Khalid
Printed by Mega Basim, Istanbul, Turkey

We would like to take the opportunity to thank all those who participated in the compilation and translation of this book in particular the brothers and sisters from the Muslim Youth League, the respected Shuyukh and brother Muhammad Khalid of MK Consultants Halifax.

بسم الله الرحمن الرحيم

In the Name of Allah, the Most Kind, the Most Merciful

CONTENTS

Introduction:
The Three *Fitan* 11

Chapter 1:
Authenticity of Traditions 19

Chapter 2:
Qur'anic Evidence for Imam Mahdi عليه السلام 27

Chapter 3:
Three Periods of the Signs of Qiyamah 33

Chapter 4:
Minor Signs of Qiyamah Present Today 45

Chapter 5:
Third Period: Major Signs of Qiyamah 57

Chapter 6:
The Personality of Imam Mahdi عليه السلام 61

Chapter 7:
Qur'anic Reference to the victory of Imam Mahdi عليه السلام 67

Chapter 8:
Events At The Time of Imam Mahdi عليه السلام 75

Chapter 9:
Twelve Final Signs of The Nearness of Qiyamah 97

Chapter 10:
The Appearance of Imam Mahdi عليه السلام 111

Bibliography 119

INTRODUCTION
THE THREE FITAN

The subject of discussion concerns the coming of Imam Muhammad Mahdi ﵇; lending focus on key and timely aspects. One may ask why there is a need to study the above subject. To understand this one must appreciate that throughout history erroneous beliefs about Imam Muhammad Mahdi ﵇ have taken shape and accumulated into a body of *fitan*. For instance one such *fitna*, resulting from the grave misunderstandings of a few contemporary scholars, recurring in different periods of time, has been the belief that no personality by the name of Imam Muhammad Mahdi ﵇ exists or will emerge. Rather a *'mahdi'* appears in every era. Such thought has provoked individuals to apply the label of *'mahdi'* to themselves and as a consequence straying from the path and leading others astray.

This belief is categorised as a *fitna* due to the fact that Imam Muhammad Mahdi ﵇ is a specific person and a unique *Imam*, whom the Holy Prophet ﷺ mentioned on several occasions, whose coming He ﷺ foretold, and about whom he gave clear details. Hence the denial and rejection of the coming of Imam Muhammad Mahdi ﵇ means drifting away from and openly rebelling against the sayings of the Holy Prophet ﷺ.

A great collection of the Holy Prophet's ﷺ traditions (Ahadith) discuss the coming of Imam Muhammad Mahdi ﵇. These include a composition of traditions of varying degrees, such as *mutawatir, marfu'*, *sahih* and *hasan*. *Da'if* (weak) traditions promoted to the level of *maqbul* (accepted) are also included because many *da'if* narrations of the same *hadith*, strengthen the authenticity of that *hadith*. In all, over two hundred traditions relating to Imam Muhammad Mahdi عليه السلام have been exhaustively studied; each one individually noted as part of the research presented before you. However the total number of traditions regarding Imam Muhammad Mahdi عليه السلام is undoubtedly greater.

It is necessary to understand that the activity of consolidating evidences dealing with the coming of Imam Muhammad Mahdi عليه السلام is not merely aggregating numbers from books, but it is careful, intricate research that delves into original sources. Which renders false or repudiates the claims that the issue of Imam Muhammad Mahdi عليه السلام is: fictitious, based on myth, or has been fabricated by Shi'as. In reality, this topic is far from fabrication, rather it is based upon knowledge transmitted to us from the Holy Prophet Muhammad ﷺ. Furthermore, there is and always has been a unanimous consensus (*ijma*) of the *Ummah (about Imam Mahdi* عليه السلام*)*: from the Companions, *Tabi'in*, the early *mujtahideen*, the scholars of the *ahl-ul-bait* to all *muhaditheen*, *fuqaha*, *ulama'*, saints and sufis of all sects and schools of thought in Islam throughout every age to the present time. The coming of Imam Mahdi عليه السلام has never been a disputed issue because in reality this topic is not one which should cause any confusion.

The only significant difference has been between the Ahlu's-Sunnah and the Shi'a quarters. The Shia believe that Imam Muhammad Mahdi عليه السلام was born, disappeared, and that he will reappear whereas the Ahlu's-Sunnah believe that Imam

Muhammad Mahdi عليه السلام has not yet been born - he will appear as Imam Muhammad Mahdi عليه السلام and announce his arrival. Apart from this single difference, no other difference in the *Ummah* regarding the appearance and status of Imam Muhammad Mahdi عليه السلام exists. In no way does this difference question the *actual* coming of Imam Muhammad Mahdi عليه السلام.

Moving on, another *fitna* which has become prevalent is where pretentious individuals, who are bold enough, claim the title of Imam Muhammad Mahdi عليه السلام for themselves. There is a complete list of such people who have appeared throughout Islamic history. However it will be sufficient to mention a contemporary claimer: Ghulam Ahmad Qadiyani, of Indian origin, falsely claimed to be the *Mahdi.* Shortly after, he promoted himself to be the Prophet Isa عليه السلام. Finally he ended his chain of self-promotions with the claim of Prophethood. Little did he know that a third personality - Dajjal - would also appear during the age of Imam Muhammad Mahdi عليه السلام, since he failed to lay a claim to the title, possibly due to no one informing him. In reality, he was neither Imam Mahdi عليه السلام, nor was he Prophet Isa عليه السلام, in reality he mirrored the Dajjal. We know from a tradition of the Holy Prophet ﷺ:

عَنْ أَبِي هُرَيْرَةَ رَضِي اللهُ عَنْهُ، عَنِ النَّبِيِّ صَلَّى اللهُ عَلَيْهِ وَآلِهِ وَسَلَّمَ، قَالَ: لَا تَقُومُ السَّاعَةُ حَتَّى يَقْتَتِلَ فِئَتَانِ، فَيَكُونُ بَيْنَهُمَا مَقْتَلَةٌ عَظِيمَةٌ دَعْوَاهُمَا وَاحِدَةٌ وَلَا تَقُومُ السَّاعَةُ حَتَّى يُبْعَثَ دَجَّالُونَ كَذَّابُونَ، قَرِيبًا مِنْ ثَلَاثِينَ، كُلُّهُمْ يَزْعُمُ أَنَّهُ رَسُولُ اللهِ۔

It is narrated by Abu Hurayrah ﷺ that the Holy Prophet ﷺ said, "The Hour will not be established till two big groups fight each other whereupon there will be a great battle between them, the assertion of faith of both is one (and the same). And the hour will not be established till about thirty Dajjals (impostures) and liars appear, and each one of them will assume that he is Allah's ﷻ Apostle.[1]

The Prophet ﷺ gave us this definition of a dajjal in a unanimously agreed tradition, recorded by both Bukhari and Muslim. Thus Ghulam Ahmad Qadiyani was clearly amongst these thirty dajjals, since he made a claim to Prophethood after he had announced himself as Imam Mahdi ؑ and Prophet Isa ؑ. History shows us that many have claimed false Prophethood and similarly there is record of those who falsely claimed to be the '*mahdi*' during their lifetime.

Now there is a third *fitnah* which has emerged whereby those

---

[1]Bukhari, as-Sahih, vol. 3, p. 1320 # 3413 & vol. 6, p. 2605 # 6704.
Muslim, as-Sahih, vol. 4, p. 2239 # 157.
Tirmidhi, as-Sunan, vol. 4, p. 498 # 2218.
Ahmad bin Hambal, al-Musnad, vol. 2, pp. 236, 313, 530 # 7227, 8122, 10877.

who are unable to consider themselves to be Imam Mahdi عليه السلام are declaring others to be him. They fear rejection from the masses if they were to lay claim to the title and clearly do not have the courage to declare it. Thus they announce and promote someone else as Imam Mahdi عليه السلام. As a consequence individuals are being awarded the esteemed position on a regular basis from country to country, around the world.

There are scholars, speakers and so-called thinkers who are writing, stating in their lectures and mentioning on television that Imam Muhammad Mahdi عليه السلام has been born. This is not an epidemic exclusive to the Indian sub-continent, but has clutched parts of the Arab world within its folds. The claims are vast and diverse involving not ordinary people but those considered as the intelligentsia. Some believe he was born in 1960, others have stated meeting him, and his residence differs from Yemen, Pakistan to Sudan. In Iraq a young boy who had memorized the entire Quran in his infancy was considered by some as Imam Mahdi عليه السلام and such reports have also appeared in Sudan. Presently, it appears that anyone who wishes to do so, finds a '*mahdi*' in one place or another.

Over the past few years these announcements have become so frequent that it has made a mockery of the true understanding of the appearance of Imam Muhammad Mahdi عليه السلام conveyed to us by the Holy Prophet ﷺ. The danger is that people accept what scholars preach to them but when the years pass and there is no sign of Imam Muhammad Mahdi عليه السلام, it can result in loss of faith or the complete rejection of such a coming. This can lead to people turning away from Islam as they question the reliability of what they have learnt from these very scholars.

Furthermore, global catastrophes such as the South East Asian tsunami and the earthquake in Pakistan or the disastrous situation in Iraq and the terrible bloodshed throughout the Middle East, are wrongly interpreted as signs signaling the coming of Imam Muhammad Mahdi عليه السلام. Therefore a comprehensive discussion will be carried out in the light of the Quran, traditions, and classical sources, so that all misconceptions related to the coming of Imam Muhammad Mahdi عليه السلام are clarified.

The urgency of addressing the topic at hand is a requirement of the times in order that the true beliefs and correct understanding surrounding the appearance of Imam Muhammad Mahdi عليه السلام are made crystal clear and to allow the future to be free from the slightest trace of these *fitan* outlined above. The purpose of this work, by the Will of Allah ﷻ, is to obliterate speculations surrounding the appearance of Imam Muhammad Mahdi عليه السلام and whether he is to appear soon or not. In the process of accomplishing this, the exact year of the appearance of Imam Muhammad Mahdi عليه السلام will be revealed as directed by the traditions of the Prophet ﷺ. The intentions are that what follows acts as a filter between what is ambiguous and what is explicit in connection to the coming of Imam Muhammad Mahdi عليه السلام.

CHAPTER ONE
AUTHENTICITY OF TRADITIONS

Here we prove the authenticity of the many traditions that discuss Imam Muhammad Mahdi عليه السلام, as well as detailing the books written by classical Imams and scholars on the subject. Imam al-Qurtubi has given the traditions on Imam Muhammad Mahdi عليه السلام the status of *mutawatir*. Imam Mizzi, who is an Imam of *asma'u'r-rijal* in the science of hadith, has also classed these traditions as *mutawatir*. According to the Shari'ah, it is *wajib* (necessary) to accept the ruling of a *mutawatir* tradition. Anyone who rejects a *mutawatir* tradition is considered to be astray. Imam Ibn al-Qayyim al-Jawzi also classed them as *mutawatir*. Imam Ibn Hajar al-Asqalani also classed them as *mutawatir* together with Imam as-Sakhawi, Imam Jalalu'd-din as-Suyuti, Imam Ibn Hajar al-Makki, Mulla Ali Qari, Imam az-Zurqani, Imam al-Qastallani and Imam al-Barzanji. All of these Imams and *Muhaditheen* accepted the traditions about the coming of Imam Muhammad Mahdi عليه السلام as being at the level of *tawatur*. In this context, it is worth bearing in mind that amongst the vast treasure trove of *ahadith* we possess, the number of traditions recognised as *mutawatir* is very small in proportion to others.

Another measure for the authenticity and acceptability of traditions, is whether or not great Imams have used them as sources for their arguments and rulings. The following Imams and *Muhaditheen* have used these traditions about Imam Muhammad Mahdi عليه السلام and have derived evidence from them in order to prove the circumstances surrounding his coming, his attributes and his high status:

- Imam Sufyan ath-Thawri, who is known as *ameer-ul-mumineen* amongst Imams of *hadith.*
- Imam Abu Ja'far Uqaidi
- Imam Ibn Hibban, author of *Sahih Ibn Hibban*
- Imam Abu Sulaiman al-Khattabi
- Imam Baihaqi
- Imam Abu'l-Qasim as-Suhaili,
- Imam Abu Abdullah al-Qurtubi
- Imam Jalalu'd-din as-Suyuti
- Imam Ibn Hajar al-Makki
- Imam Ali al-Muttaqi al-Hindi, author of *Kanz-ul-Ummal*
- Imam Abdu'r-Rauf al-Manawi.
- Allama Ibn Taymiyyah
- Imam Ibn al-Qayyim al-Jawzi
- Imam Ibn Kathir.

The latter three Imams are considered by some to represent an extreme anti-Sufi position, yet they too have accepted these traditions as a *hujjah.*

The former Grand Mufti of Saudi Arabia, Shaykh Abdal-Aziz ibn Baaz, also accepted these traditions as a *hujjah.* The present position of the scholars of Saudi Arabia is that they only accept one *muhaddith* - Shaykh Nasir ad-Din al-Bani - as being a *hujjah* in the *tahqeeq* and *takhreej* of traditions. They only acknowledge his research as being authoritative, accepting nobody else's. They do not commonly print the research of anyone else. Shaykh Nasir ad-Din al-Bani has also accepted the traditions about Imam Muhammad Mahdi عليه السلام as being authentic.

Books written by Imams on Imam Mahdi عليه السلام

The next step in determining the authenticity of the reports concerning the coming of Imam Muhammad Mahdi عليه السلام is to examine the books written and compiled by the classical Imams on the subject. *Muhaditheen* and Imams have written books about Imam Muhammad Mahdi عليه السلام and have compiled collections of traditions on the subject. The first among them is Imam Nu'aym ibn Hammad (d. 228 AH) who was the Shaykh of: Imam al-Bukhari, Imam Muslim, Imam at-Tirmidhi, Imam Abu Dawud, Imam Ibn Majah and Imam an-Nasa'i. All the Imams responsible for the *Sihah Sitta* narrated traditions from him. Imam Nu'aym ibn Hammad wrote books on Imam Muhammad Mahdi عليه السلام and compiled treatises on him عليه السلام. In his book *Kitabu'l-Fitan* he collected traditions on *Akhbar al-Mahdi* (Reports about the Mahdi).

Imam Abdu'r-Razzaq ibn Hammam (d. 211 AH); a student of Imam Abu Hanifah and the Shaykh in Hadith of Imam al-Bukhari, also collected traditions on Imam Muhammad Mahdi عليه السلام. Imam Abu Bakr ibn Abi Shaybah (d. 235 AH) who was a Shaykh of: Imam al-Bukhari, Imam Ibn Majah, Imam Abu Dawud, Imam at-Tirmidhi, Imam Ibn Khuzaymah and Imam Ibn Hibban; all wrote treatises on Imam Muhammad Mahdi عليه السلام including traditions relating to him. These are the roots, sources, and fountains of the treasure of knowledge which is available in the books of Hadith concerning Imam Muhammad Mahdi عليه السلام.

The following Imams also compiled books of traditions about Imam Muhammad Mahdi عليه السلام:

- Imam Ibn Abi Khuzayma
- Imam Habbab ibn Ya'qub
- Imam Abul Husayn Ahmad bin Ja'far
- Imam Abu Nu'aym al-Isfahani
- Imam Muhammad ibn Yusuf ash-Shafi'i
- Imam Ibn al-Qayyim al-Jawzi
- Imam Ibn Kathir
- Imam as-Sakhawi
- Imam Jalalu'd-din as-Suyuti
- Imam Ahmad ibn Hajar al-Makki
- Imam Ali al-Muttaqi al-Hindi, author of *Kanz-ul-Ummal*
- Mulla Ali Qari

A full list of those who have written books on Imam Muhammad Mahdi عليه السلام cannot be given here due to constraints of space, but such a list is available together with some of the actual books concerned. The names given above are sufficient to make it crystal clear that the existence of Imam Muhammad Mahdi عليه السلام and his coming is an issue that is given high status and importance by the *Deen* of Islam, the *Shari'ah* of the Prophet

Muhammad ﷺ, and the entire vast corpus of Hadith literature.

Qadi Muhammad ibn Ali as-Shawkani, compiled a whole book of traditions about Imam Muhammad Mahdi عليه السلام. He is accepted as an Imam by the *Salafis* and relied upon by scholars of the *Ahlu'l-hadith* and Saudi Arabia. Nawab Siddiq Hassan Khan Bawpali, another highly regarded *Ahlu'l-hadith* scholar, also compiled traditions on Imam Muhammad Mahdi عليه السلام, classing them as *mutawatir*.

These references to so many Imams clearly indicate that the issue of Imam Muhammad Mahdi is not one that has been fabricated by Shi'a scholars and Ja'fari *fiqh*. A major problem arises when some people start to make rebuttals on the basis of sectarian differences. Whilst doing so, they at the same time refute and negate true facts and realities without distinguishing them from actual fallacies and fabrications. Fuelled by enmity and rivalry, these people reject everything and as a result they transgress the limits. It is essential to not allow sectarian differences to destroy faith and the true criteria of belief. *Haqq* (truth) is always *haqq*. *Haqq* is not something which can be used merely to back up a particular viewpoint nor can it be rejected out of enmity towards a particular person. Belief in *haqq* as being *haqq* is in fact nothing other than what is known as *iman* (true belief).

CHAPTER TWO
QUR'ANIC EVIDENCE RELATING TO IMAM MAHDI عليه السلام

Here Quranic evidence for Imam Mahdi will be presented, followed by a detailed examination of traditions on the subject. Imams of *tafsir* have discussed the coming of Imam Muhammad Mahdi whilst referring to a particular Quranic verse. Allah states in Sura al-Baqarah:

وَمَنْ أَظْلَمُ مِمَّنْ مَنَعَ مَسَاجِدَ اللَّهِ أَنْ يُذْكَرَ فِيهَا اسْمُهُ وَسَعَىٰ فِي خَرَابِهَا أُولَٰئِكَ
مَا كَانَ لَهُمْ أَنْ يَدْخُلُوهَا إِلَّا خَائِفِينَ لَهُمْ فِي الدُّنْيَا خِزْيٌ وَلَهُمْ فِي الْآخِرَةِ
عَذَابٌ عَظِيمٌ O

> *"And who is more unjust than he who forbids remembering of Allah's name in His mosques and strives to desolate them? It was not proper for them to enter the mosques except that they were in the state of fearing (Allah). For them is disgrace in this world and a dreadful torment (also awaits them) in the Hereafter."* [1]

This verse has two applications. The first is the common application of teaching for the *ummah* and the second is directly tied to the historical circumstances of its revelation. Imam as-Suddi al-Kabir, who was a student of Abdullah Ibn Abbas and a

---

[1] Qur'an (*al-Baqarah*), 2: 114.

high ranking *Tabi'i*, gave an interpretation and explanation of the circumstances behind the revelation of this verse. This was quoted by Imam Ibn Jarir at-Tabari in his *Tafsir*. Ibn Jarir and many Imams of *tafsir* used this explanation in their *tafsirs*, including Imam Jalalu'd-din as-Suyuti who is one of the greatest authorities among the Ahl-us-Sunnah Imams of *tafsir*.

عَنِ السَّدِّيِ قَوْلُهُ: لَهُمْ فِي الدُّنْيَا خِزْيٌ أَمَّا خِزْيُهُمْ فِي الدُّنْيَا، فَإِنَّهُمْ إِذَا قَامَ الْمَهْدِيُ وَفُتِحَتِ الْقُسْطُنْطِينِيَّةُ قَتَلَهُمْ، فَذَلِكَ الْخِزْيُ، وَأَمَّا عَذَابٌ عَظِيمٌ فَإِنَّهُ عَذَابُ جَهَنَّمَ الَّذِي لَا يُخَفَّفُ عَنْ أَهْلِهِ، وَلَا يُقْضَى عَلَيْهِمْ فِيهَا فَيَمُوتُوا.

"As-Suddi said: Allah Almighty said, "For them is disgrace in this world," they will be disgraced when Imam Mahdi will come and Constantinople will be conquered, he will kill them and this is the disgrace. As far as the big torment is concerned, it will be the torment of hell which will not be reduced. Nor shall they be killed in it (Hell) so that they die." [2]

When Nebuchadnazzar (Babylonian King) was victorious, he emptied out *Baitu'l-Maqdis* (also known as *al-Quds* and Jerusalem), along with the prayer places and put a stop to prayers and the remembrance of Allah ﷻ.

Imam Suddi al-Kabir says that this verse refers to the Romans.

---

[2] Tabari, Jami-ul-bayan fi tafsir-il-Qur'an, vol. 1, p. 501.
Suyuti, ad-Durr-ul-manthur fit-tafsir bil-ma'thur, vol. 1, p. 264.
Shawkani, Fath-ul-qadir, vol. 1, p. 132.

Referring to the next part of the verse, he says that those Romans who banned the remembrance of Allah ﷻ from His houses during the time of the Roman Empire could then only enter *Baitu'l-Maqdis* fearfully with their heads bowed.

At the present time, Jerusalem is in the hands of Jews and today it is the Muslims who are fearful and enter with their heads bowed, there is no restriction on "Romans", meaning Europeans or Christians in general. Imam Ibn Jarir at-Tabari narrates from Imam as-Suddi al-Kabir that, since the "Romans" are no longer fearful, nor do they enter with their heads bowed, then which period of time does this part of the verse apply? The verse further states that they (the Romans) will be suffering great hardship at that time due to being punished for the oppression they carried out in the past. Imam Suddi al-Kabir, narrating from Imam Abdullah Ibn Abbas ؓ, stated clearly that this verse is referring to the time when Imam Muhammad Mahdi ﷺ will come.

Imam Muhammad Mahdi ﷺ will conquer Jerusalem and Constantinople (modern day Istanbul). Jerusalem will be the capital city of his global state. This refers to a time when Imam Muhammad Mahdi ﷺ will be the head of an Islamic state and the last Caliph and Imam of the *ummah* of Prophet Muhammad ﷺ. So this verse is referring to a time when the "Romans" will once more enter *Baitu'l-Maqdis* in fear and to seek peace. In this way, before the presentation of a large amount of traditions on the subject, Quranic evidence derived from a verse in the Qur'an, accompanied by its interpretation by a high ranking *Tabi'i,* and related by Imam Ibn Jarir at-Tabari as well as many other Imams, has been presented.

CHAPTER THREE
THREE PERIODS OF THE SIGNS OF QIYAMAH

A very important point that must be understood is that the coming of Imam Muhammad Mahdi عليه السلام is one of the signs of *Qiyamah.* There are three periods for the signs of the Day of Judgment also known as *ashratu's-sa'ah* or *alamatu qiyami's-sa'ah.* The first period began with the passing away of the Prophet ﷺ and ended about a thousand years later. The passing away of the Holy Prophet ﷺ was the first of the signs of *Qiyamah.* When the Holy Prophet ﷺ performed the great miracle of splitting the moon into two, the Quran announced:

اقْتَرَبَتِ السَّاعَةُ وَانشَقَّ الْقَمَرُ ﴿١﴾

The Hour (of Judgment) is nigh, and the moon is cleft asunder [1]

So the nearness of *Qiyamah* was first announced by the Prophet ﷺ in his lifetime. The second period of the signs of *Qiyamah* will contain the minor signs of *Qiyamah* known as *ashratu's-sa'ah as-sughra.* The second period is well underway, with the present era laying within it. The final period is yet to come.

Traditions will be presented on all three periods. There is no time limit suggesting when this second period of the signs of

---

[1] Qur'an (al-Qamar), 54: 1

Qiyamah is going to end. A thorough study of the large quantity of traditions relating to Imam Muhammad Mahdi with attention given to the relevant historical factors and contextual materials has not been carried out before. People tend to study the traditions in isolation and consequently make mistakes and become misguided, which has resulted in the spread of the *fitnah* referred to earlier. It is important to point out that Imam Muhammad Mahdi will not appear during the period of the minor signs of *Qiyamah,* which is currently in progress. Anyone who claims to be Imam Muhammad Mahdi during this period can only be considered a liar and a *dajjal.* People who announce others to be the *Mahdi* during this period are either very ignorant of, or oblivious to the correct knowledge of the *Deen.* Nothing more can be said of such people. When this period of the minor signs of *Qiyamah* ends, the third period will begin. That will be the period of the major signs of *Qiyamah* known as *amaratu's-sa'ah al-kubra.*

Another significant point is that such an important event as the coming of Imam Muhammad Mahdi could never take place during a time of minor signs. It is a logical point that such a major personality could only appear at a time of major *fitnah* in the *ummah.* At times of minor *fitan* and disruptions, only minor personalities appear. The first major sign of *Qiyamah,* marking the beginning of the third period, will in fact be the coming of Imam Muhammad Mahdi.

There is a clear difference between the three periods. Imam Tabarani related that Abdullah ibn Umar said that the passing away of the Holy Prophet ﷺ was the first sign of the nearness of *Qiyamah*. The second sign would be the passing away of all of the Companions. There was a not a single Companion still alive in the second century AH.

عَنْ عَلِيٍّ رَضِيَ اللهُ عَنْهُ، قَالَ: قَالَ رَسُولُ اللهِ صَلَّى اللهُ عَلَيْهِ وَآلِهِ وَسَلَّمَ: لَا تَقُومُ السَّاعَةُ حَتَّى يُلْتَمَسَ رَجُلٌ مِنْ أَصْحَابِي، كَمَا تُلْتَمَسُ الضَّالَّةُ، فَلَا يُوجَدُ.

> *"Narrated by 'Ali ﷺ that the Messenger of Allah ﷺ said, "The Hour will not come until one of my Companions will be looked for in the same way as (somebody looks for his) lost/missing chattel. But none will be found (because they all will have gone)."* [2]

Sayyiduna Ali ﷺ reported that the Holy Prophet ﷺ said that *Qiyamah* would not come until all his Companions were gone from this world. A time would come when a search will be carried out to look for a single Companion just like a search is carried out to find a lost item, but even then no Companion would be found (ref Imam Ahmad bin Hanbal, Musnad.). Other *fitan* of that time such as the martyrdom of Sayyidina Uthman ibn Affan , the third orthodox caliph, and the massacre of Karbala,

[2] Ahmad bin Hambal, al-Musnad, vol. 1, p. 89, 93 # 675, 720.
Ibn 'Adi transmitted in al-Kamil, vol. 1, p. 425 and said it mustaqim al-hadith.
Haythami, Majma'-uz-zawa'id, vol. 10, p. 18.
Haythami said that Ahmad and Bazzar had transmitted it.

were also signs of *Qiyamah* during the first period of the signs of *Qiyamah.*

عَنْ حُذَيْفَةَ قَالَ: أَوَّلُ الْفِتَنِ قَتْلُ عُثْمَانَ، وَآخِرُهَا خُرُوجُ الدَّجَّالِ۔

"Hudhaifa ﷺ narrates that Allah's Messenger ﷺ said, "The first of the seditions is the murder of Uthman and the last one is the appearance of Dajjal." [3]

The following tradition, which many people will be reading for the first time, illustrates the knowledge of the Unseen possessed by the Holy Prophet Muhammad ﷺ and the extent to which Allah ﷻ revealed secrets of the Unseen to him ﷺ. In this tradition, the Holy Prophet ﷺ mentioned events that would take place during the first period, such as the Tartar *fitnah* which took place approximately six hundred and fifty years after the time of the Prophet ﷺ in Baghdad. The Mongols – the Tartar people who were led by Hulagu Khan, the grandson of Genghis khan, attacked Baghdad in 1258 C.E and brought the Abbasid caliphate to an end.

The Mongols massacred two million, three hundred thousand Muslims in the process and the water in the river Tigris turned red for three days with the blood of Muslims. Power was wrested from the Muslims and because of this there was no Islamic state

---

[3] Ibn Abd-ul-Barr, al-Istidhkar, vol. 8, p. 519 # 1826.
Ibn Asakir in Tarikh Dimash al-Kabir, vol. 39, p. 447.
Hindi, Kanz-ul-Ummal, vol. 6, p. 2605 # 6701.

on the face of the earth for a period of fifty years. This was the biggest *fitnah* in the history of Islam. It was the greatest massacre and the worst example of oppression in the history of the *Ummah*, a horrific event without precedent. Many of us have read about this event in history books but very few are aware that the Holy Prophet ﷺ mentioned it in detail over six centuries earlier. This is a tradition of Sahih al-Bukhari that is also in Sahih Muslim, Sunan Abu Dawud, at-Tirmidhi and Ibn Majah. The Prophet ﷺ said:

عَنْ أَبِي هُرَيْرَةَ رَضِيَ اللَّهُ عَنْهُ، عَنِ النَّبِيِّ صَلَّى اللَّهُ عَلَيْهِ وَآلِهِ وَسَلَّمَ، قَالَ: لَا تَقُومُ السَّاعَةُ حَتَّى تُقَاتِلُوا قَوْمًا نِعَالُهُمُ الشَّعَرُ، وَلَا تَقُومُ السَّاعَةُ حَتَّى تُقَاتِلُوا قَوْمًا، كَأَنَّ وُجُوهَهُمُ الْمَجَانُّ الْمُطْرَقَةُ. وَفِي رِوَايَةٍ: صِغَارَ الْأَعْيُنِ، ذُلْفَ الْأُنُوفِ، كَأَنَّ وُجُوهَهُمُ الْمَجَانُّ الْمُطْرَقَةُ

"Narrated Abu Hurayrah: The Prophet ﷺ said, "The Hour will not be established till you fight with people wearing shoes made of hair. And the Hour will not be established till you fight with people whose faces will be as if they are (covered with) tough and battered (leather-like skin)."

"And in another tradition, "(They will be) small-eyed, small and flat-nosed, and their faces will be as if they are (covered with) tough and bartered (leather-like skin)." [4]

---

[4] Agreed upon by Bukhari and Muslim.

In another version in *Kanz-ul-Ummal* it is said that they will be from the lineage of Kantura. Kantura was a female slave and the Tartars are descended from her children. The *muhaditheen* are unanimous in their agreement that this tradition refers to the events of 656 AH, which corresponds to 1258 CE, in other words the Tartar attack on Baghdad. So this great event in history comes within the first period of the signs of *Qiyamah.*

The next tradition is from Sahih Bukhari narrated by Abu Hurayrah ﷺ and Abu Dharr which Imam al-Hakim, in his book *Mustadrak*, classed as *sahih*. It is also in at-Tabarani and *Majma' az-Zawa'id* transmitted by Asim ibn Ali al-Ansari.

عَنْ أَبِي هُرَيْرَةَ أَنَّ رَسُولَ اللهِ صَلَّى اللهُ عَلَيْهِ وَآلِهِ وَسَلَّمَ قَالَ: لَا تَقُومُ السَّاعَةُ
حَتَّى تَخْرُجَ نَارٌ مِنْ أَرْضِ الْحِجَازِ، تُضِيءُ أَعْنَاقَ الْإِبِلِ بِبُصْرَى.

Abu Hurayrah ﷺ narrates that the Messenger of Allah said, "The Hour will not be established till a fire will come out of the land of Hijaz, and it will light up the necks of the camels at Busra."[5]

Qiyamah will not take place until a great fire rages near Madinah

---

Bukhari, as-Sahih, vol. 3, pp. 1071, 1316 # 2771, 3397.
Muslim, as-Sahih, vol. 4, pp. 2233-2234 # 2912.
Tirmidhi graded it hasan (fair) sahih (sound) in al-Jami'-us-sahih, vol. 4, p. 497, # 2215.

[5] Unanimously agreed upon by Bukhari and Muslim.
Bukhari, as-Sahih, vol. 6, p. 2605, # 6701.
Muslim, as-Sahih, vol. 4, p. 2227 # 2902.
'Abd-ur-Razzaq, al-Musannaf, vol. 11, p. 376 # 20788.

in the Hijaz. The fire will engulf the whole region and will rage so violently that the heads of camels in caravans travelling in the Syrian city of Busra will be seen by the light created by that inferno. That fire will light up the whole region up to Greater Syria so that night will appear to be midday. This fire that the Prophet ﷺ mentioned in the hadith, saying it would take place before the time of *Qiyamah*, also took place in 654 AH.

These two great events, about which the Holy Prophet ﷺ informed us, took place in close proximity to one another. On one side the caliphate in Baghdad was overthrown, with the Tartar *fitnah* wiping out every trace of Islam, destroying it with the open slaughter of two million, three hundred thousand Muslims. The Tartar army, coming from Mongolia, passed through and conquered Iran before attacking Baghdad. During the same period, there was another historic event. There was an earthquake in Madinah in 654 AH. The earthquake struck on a Tuesday night in the month of *Jumada al-Ula* and lasted for three to four days. It set off the fire that lit up the whole region up to Busra. Imam Abu Shama, Imam Qastalani and Imam Qurtubi wrote that people in Damascus saw that fire, which had been mentioned by the Holy Prophet ﷺ. This fire became a historical fact and is mentioned in history books. The world witnessed the fire that the Prophet ﷺ had mentioned six centuries earlier.

In the same way, we find in *Sahih al-Bukhari* another hadith from the Prophet ﷺ:

عَنْ أَبِي هُرَيْرَةَ رَضِيَ اللهُ عَنْهُ، عَنِ النَّبِيِّ صَلَّى اللهُ عَلَيْهِ وَآلِهِ وَسَلَّمَ، قَالَ: لَا تَقُومُ السَّاعَةُ حَتَّى يَقْتَتِلَ فِئَتَانِ، فَيَكُونَ بَيْنَهُمَا مَقْتَلَةٌ عَظِيمَةٌ دَعْوَاهُمَا وَاحِدَةٌ وَلَا تَقُومُ السَّاعَةُ حَتَّى يُبْعَثَ دَجَّالُونَ كَذَّابُونَ، قَرِيبًا مِنْ ثَلَاثِينَ، كُلُّهُمْ يَزْعُمُ أَنَّهُ رَسُولُ اللهِ.

It is narrated by Abu Hurayrah ﷺ that the Holy Prophet ﷺ said, "The Hour will not be established till two big groups fight each other whereupon there will be a great battle between them, the assertion of faith of both is one (and the same). And the hour will not be established till about thirty Dajjals (impostures) and liars appear, and each one of them will assume that he is Allah's Apostle. [6]

عَنْ حُذَيْفَةَ أَنَّ نَبِيَّ اللهِ صَلَّى اللهُ عَلَيْهِ وَآلِهِ وَسَلَّمَ قَالَ: فِي أُمَّتِي كَذَّابُونَ وَدَجَّالُونَ سَبْعَةٌ وَعِشْرُونَ، مِنْهُمْ أَرْبَعُ نِسْوَةٍ وَإِنِّي خَاتَمُ النَّبِيِّينَ، لَا نَبِيَّ بَعْدِي.

"Hudhaifa ﷺ narrated that the Holy Prophet ﷺ said, "There will be 27 liars and Dajjal (impostors) in my Ummah; four of them will be women. Whereas (the fact is that) I am the last Prophet and there will be no prophet after me." [7]

---

[6] Agreed upon by al-Bukhari and Muslim.
Bukhari, as-Sahih, vol. 3, p. 1320 # 3413 & vol. 6, p. 2605 # 6704.
Muslim, as-Sahih, vol. 4, p. 2239 # 157.
Tirmidhi, as-Sunan, vol. 4, p. 498 # 2218.
Ahmad bin Hambal, al-Musnad, vol. 2, pp. 236, 313, 530 # 7227, 8122, 10877.
[7] Ahmad bin Hambal, al-Musnad, vol. 5, p. 396 # 23406.

The last *dajjal* out of these thirty will be the one who comes at the time of Prophet Isa ﷺ and Imam Muhammad Mahdi ﷺ. He will also say that he is a Prophet, this will be his first claim. Once he has convinced people of this, he will then make a second claim that he is God. The Prophet ﷺ said there would also be women '*kadhdhab dajjal*' claimants of Prophethood and they would number four.

These examples taken from traditions make it clear that the first period of the signs of *Qiyamah*, lasted from the passing away of the Prophet ﷺ until somewhere between 800 and 1000 AH. This was the first period of *fitan*. After that the second period, consisting of the minor signs of *Qiyamah*, began.

Why people are confused

Those people who have announced the coming of Imam Muhammad Mahdi ﷺ have made the mistake of not distinguishing between the period of the minor signs of *Qiyamah* and that of the major signs. They have merely had a general understanding of the fact that a few major incidents or signs will take place before *Qiyamah*. They discuss the traditions that mention these signs which are commonly known and frequently mentioned by scholars. As a result of this they arrive at the

---

Tabarani, al-Mujam-ul-kabir, vol. 3, p. 169 # 3026.
Tabarani, al-Mujam-ul-awsat, vol. 5, p. 327 # 5450.
Daylami, Musnad al-Firdaws, vol. 5, p. 454 # 8724.

conclusion that these signs have already appeared, implying therefore, that the time of Imam Muhammad Mahdi عليه السلام has also arrived. This is where the confusion comes into being. Whereas the truth is that, as we have seen, this is in fact the era of the minor signs of *Qiyamah.* The exact time when this period will end is best known by Allah ﷻ and His Messenger ﷺ.

The third period of *fitan*, the major signs of *Qiyamah*, will then commence. There will be twelve major signs of *Qiyamah*, ten of which will come at once. The first of those twelve signs and the beginning of the major signs of *Qiyamah* will be the coming of Imam Muhammad Mahdi عليه السلام.

In summary there are three periods of signs leading up to *Qiyamah*: the first period of signs and *fitan*, which lasted from the passing away of the Prophet ﷺ for approximately a thousand years, the second period of signs and *fitan* which are now underway, known as the Minor Signs of *Qiyamah*, and the third period of signs and *fitan*, which has yet to arrive, known as the Major Signs of *Qiyamah*.

CHAPTER FOUR
MINOR SIGNS OF QIYAMAH PRESENT TODAY

Some incidents and events that are signs of Qiyamah and exist at the present time have caused confusion. They are discussed in many traditions.

> *The Prophet ﷺ said that the signs of the coming of Qiyamah will be that it will rain abundantly but harvests will return very little. There will be many who study and speak about the Holy Quran and Islam but very few will actually understand them. There will be many wealthy people but very few will be reliable and trustworthy.* [1]

The Prophet ﷺ also said that before Qiyamah people would adopt piety, modesty, *taqwa*, talk of Islamic spirituality and mysticism, all as a matter of custom and ritual only. People will artificially adopt the physical appearance of spirituality, piety and *taqwa*. This can be seen in some present day self-proclaimed spiritual leaders who have adopted this form of life merely as a means of earning a living. They are not spiritual leaders nor do they have anything to do with *tasawwuf*, *tazkiyyah* or *ihsan*. These people have transformed the true Islamic concepts of *tasawwuf*, *zuhd*, *wara*, *taqwah*, *ruhaniyyah*, *wilayah*, *tasbih*, *dhikr* etc, into mere ritual and customs. They have only adopted the artificial outward

---

[1] Tabarani, *Majma-uz-Zawaid* #7 and #331

appearance of these concepts, which form the subject matter of their lectures, but their inner selves are empty. The true Sufis adopt the spiritual and practical aspects of these concepts and do not necessarily have any particular outward appearance.

> *On the authority of Abu Hurayrah ﷺ, the Prophet ﷺ said that men will also start to wear silky and feminine clothes. Trade and wealth will be flourishing but people will complain of the lack of barakah (i.e. people will not be content, as resources will not be deemed to be sufficient to fulfill their needs). People will be respected according to their wealth.* [2]

Respect will not be determined by knowledge, *taqwa* or conduct, but by the attraction and appeal of wealth. The Prophet ﷺ said that there would be an increase in indecency and immorality. One form of this is in the manner of dress. The Holy Prophet ﷺ said that women will try to wear male clothing and have masculine hair styles while men will try to adopt feminine fashions. Many Muslims overstep the limits of modest dress in the name of 'fashion'. 'Fashion' seems to have become an acceptable measure but in reality it is opening the doors of indecency. As a result head scarves are disappearing, revealing clothing, or clothing that bares parts of the body have become common and this is nothing but a manifestation and embodiment

---

[2] *Hilyatu'l-awliya*, Abu Nua'ym al-Isfahani

of immorality and indecency. Dresses are so revealing these days that a respectable person cannot raise his eyes and look at their wearers. Clothes are supposed to serve the purpose of concealing the body not revealing it. Such clothing deprives people of modesty, spirituality and God-consciousness. This is a great present day *fitnah* facing Muslims. In a tradition from *Sahih Muslim*, narrated by Abu Hurayrah ﷺ, the Holy Prophet ﷺ said that women would no longer cover their heads. This also refers to those women whose bodies are revealed by their clothing. Such women, even if they are not completely involved in sin and *fitnah* are nevertheless influenced by it, are in favour of it and want to be involved in it. The Prophet ﷺ said that these women will not enter paradise nor will they be anywhere near it.

The Holy Prophet ﷺ said that indecency and immorality will become so common that a time will come when women walking in the street would be set upon by some people on sight, in the way that wolves attack their prey in the middle of the road. People will say to the rapists, "Why have you attacked her in the middle of the path; you should at least have taken her to one side." People's hearts will be similar to those of wolves.

The Holy Prophet ﷺ said that at the end of time women will be greater in number than men. Traders and shopkeepers will defraud shoppers, especially by short-changing them or giving them less than they are paying for. Old people will not be respected by young people and children will not be shown mercy, compassion and love. People will be oblivious to the fact that the majority of their offspring are illegitimate, presuming their children to be their own whilst in reality they shall have been fathered by another person.

Then the Holy Prophet ﷺ said that close relations will be cut off. People will complain that their close relations do not care about them. People will not care if brothers, sisters or close relations are poor and in need; nobody will care about their poverty. The poor and needy will be wandering from door to door but they will not be provided with any charity.

Then Holy Prophet ﷺ said that property will be unlawfully confiscated from people. People will be murdered on a regular basis. The study and understanding of the Holy Quran will be deemed an inconvenience. Islam will become impoverished, meaning that those who are supposed to be Muslims will cease to practice Islam. Enmity and jealousy will spread among people, knowledge will be taken away and life expectancy will decrease.

The Prophet ﷺ said at that time liars will be proclaimed to be truthful and the truthful, liars. The dishonest and insincere will be considered honest and trustworthy. The unreliable and corrupt will be given governance and power; it is they who will be selected and elected as rulers and heads of state. On the other hand the truthful and trustworthy will be falsely accused of wrongdoing. Not a finger will be lifted against the corrupt and fraudulent, but trustworthy and truthful people will face serious allegations of wrong doing.

The Holy Prophet ﷺ said that among the signs of *Qiyamah* is that people who have been given great knowledge by Allah ﷻ and are truly knowledgeable will not be followed. They will be listened to, but they and their message will not be accepted. Those who have the attributes of self-discipline, restraint and moderation, will not have the respect of other people on that account. No matter how great a rank someone has been given by Allah ﷻ, he or she will not be respected accordingly. Murder and bloodshed will be common. People will kill each other for the sake of worldly pursuits and possessions. It is stated in a hadith that a time will come when scholars will be killed just as dogs are killed and exterminated.

Houses and residences will be huge. Children will be disobedient to their parents. Rebellion, jealousy and the inability to accommodate others will be commonplace. Ignorance and telling lies will be commonplace, whereas speaking the truth will be a rarity. Differences between people will intensify and it will be common for people to think badly of others. Preachers will lie in their sermons and the Prophet ﷺ said that they would become the most evil group of people in his *ummah*. They will praise the rich and wealthy in their sermons in order to receive monetary benefits from them. The Holy Prophet ﷺ also said that three things would become extremely rare: *halal* earning, truly beneficial knowledge, and love and friendship for the sake of Allah ﷻ alone.

Many of the things which the Prophet ﷺ told us about have already taken place, many more are taking place now, and all of them certainly will take place and be proven. We should perhaps pause here for an instant and ask whether the Holy Prophet ﷺ was happy in saying all this, or was he in fact saddened by what was going to happen to his *ummah*? It is quite clear that it must have been a great burden on the heart of the Holy Prophet ﷺ to have to describe all these atrocities, injustices and *fitan* that were going take place in his *ummah*; the losses, the destruction, the immorality and indecency, *iman* being destroyed, shame ceasing to exist, and actions becoming destructive.

The Holy Prophet ﷺ said that the time will come when men will get married to men. There will be homosexual and unisexual societies. Laws allowing single sex marriages are being passed today in the Western world. Parliaments in various countries have passed such laws. There are gay enclaves springing up in these countries and this practice will become very common in the West. Once this curse has become commonplace in the West, rulers in the Muslim world will also follow suit, as they have chosen a slavish imitation of the West for the *ummah.* Whatever is common in the West is adopted in the Muslim world in the name of 'fashion'.

These so-called Muslim rulers, who can only be considered enemies of Islam, are in fact appointed agents of the oppressive Zionist and Imperialist powers and have only been appointed to cut *iman* from its roots, to eliminate a true Islamic identity and Islamic thought and to consequently eradicate the Islamic conscience. They want the state of the Muslims to be reduced to that of the Christians, which is to go to the mosque for worship on Fridays only, just as the Christians go to church on Sunday, and otherwise leave the mosques abandoned and deserted. They also want to portray people who speak of Islamic conscience and what is *halal* and haram as fools. So that those who speak of the teachings of the Prophet ﷺ will be swept aside by saying that they are nothing but people living in the past.

These practices will be introduced into the Muslim World through the use of media. Dramas etc featuring single sex relationships will be shown. In response to public objections, the ministries responsible for doing this will claim that they are merely showing these dramas to inform 'our people' of the evil acts that are perpetrated in the West. These dramas will be shown daily, continually attacking and eliminating any remaining conscience, morality and God-consciousness in the people. The dramas will in fact have the aim of encouraging people to carry out such acts themselves. They will serve the purpose of softening the ground for the acceptance of these perverted practices in Muslim countries.

When it is seen that no violent adverse reaction in society to this indecency and immorality has occurred, these acts will be allowed to be carried out as isolated incidents. Once it is seen that the isolated incidents have not caused a bad reaction, these acts will be permitted on the basis of freedom of choice. Governments will declare it to be a private matter and nothing to do with the state. In this way, the Muslim World will be overcome by this wave of *kufr*.

Thus it can be seen that the doorway to the greatest *kufr*, the greatest immorality, the greatest indecency and the greatest destruction and annihilation of *iman* and *deen* in the world today, *is* contemporary television programming. People nowadays do not have the will-power to ensure that only religious, news and educational programs are viewed in their homes. The TV is the path of destruction for children. Nowadays people do not need to go out of their homes to access fitna; everything is admitted into the safety and comfort of their own home thanks to the TV.

The internet is used for the very same purpose. Why do children generally not use the internet in the living room that can be accessed by their parents? These 'traditional type' parents are for the most part totally oblivious of what is going on and are ignorant of the world they live in. Seventy-five percent of children make fools of their parents. Parents are also party to this destruction by considering the children of other people to be 'bad' and considering their own to be 'angelic'. It is this very frame of mind that is the cause of so much of the destruction. Such parents have no idea how their children are shredding their respect, identity and Islamic conscience to pieces.

It is our bounden duty to bring such matters to the forefront because by not doing so would risk incurring the unhappiness of the Holy Prophet ﷺ by not portraying the *haqq* as *haqq*. It does not matter whether people are offended by this action or not. It certainly is not our duty to please the creation at the expense of disobeying the teachings of the Holy Prophet ﷺ. Since the creation has no power to bring benefit, one should only seek to satisfy the Prophet ﷺ, the source of all goodness to humanity. It certainly is our duty to satisfy the Prophet ﷺ, the master and distributor - *al-Qasim*.

Therefore there is a need for people to take heed and mend

their ways so that *fitnah* and 'fashion' can be nipped in the bud. Children can only be expected to follow suit if parents and older siblings set an example by disassociating themselves from such practices. The Prophet ﷺ said about those who are on this path, that their prayers and fasting will not be accepted unless they truly repent with *tawbatu'n-nasuha*.

The Holy Prophet ﷺ further said that people will drink alcohol, legal limits will be overstepped, oaths will be unfulfilled and promises will be broken. The Qur'an will be printed very beautifully, mosques will be beautified immensely and minbars and minarets will be very beautiful and very tall but there will be enmity and gross mistrust in people's hearts. There will be many who will lecture on and teach the Holy Qur'an and Islam but those who understand it will be very few in number, and those who act upon it even fewer.

From these traditions we are able to recognise the minor signs of *Qiyamah* and after examining these *fitnahs* of the second period of the signs of *Qiyamah*, it is worth pausing and assessing contemporary society and observing whether these *fitnahs* are now rampant in our day to day lives or not. The Holy Prophet ﷺ said that they will enter into every household.

There are two concurrent paths which we can take. One is the path of fighting these *fitnahs* and waging jihad against them, and the other is being involved in them and falling prey to them. This latter path is the path leading to the *Dajjal*, who will be the imam of these *fitnahs*. Jihad against these *fitnahs* and combating them to safeguard *iman*, morality and the *Deen will be the mission of* Imam

Muhammad Mahdi ﷺ. This is the path leading to the Holy Prophet ﷺ. It is a duty for all Muslims to wage war on these *fitnahs*.

Some of the signs mentioned above, of the second period of the signs of *Qiyamah*, have not yet taken place. When all these signs have taken place only then can we expect the third period of the signs of *Qiyamah* to begin.

CHAPTER FIVE
THIRD PERIOD: MAJOR SIGNS OF QIYAMAH

The second period will be succeeded by the third and the final period, which will be marked by the appearance of Imam Mahdi ﵇. Other signs of the third and final period will occur during the time of Imam Mahdi ﵇, so therefore these signs are good indicators of whether or not the present era is the time in which Imam Mahdi ﵇ is to come.

The emergence of Imam Mahdi ﵇ will undoubtedly coincide with the appearance of Prophet Isa ﵇ and the *dajjal* as is stated in Prophetic traditions.

Prophet Isa ﵇ will descend from the heavens in al-Quds at dawn, where he will meet Imam Muhammad Mahdi ﵇ who will then lead people in *fajr* prayer.

Imam Muhammad Mahdi ﵇ will withdraw from the imam's prayer place and ask Prophet Isa ﵇ to lead the prayer instead, but upon declining Prophet Isa ﵇ will say, 'Only the imam of the *ummah* should lead the *ummah* in prayer.'

After the prayer they will open a gate to the West and encounter the *dajjal*. He will have an army of thirty thousand Jews behind him and this is where the battle will begin. Prophet Isa ﵇ and Imam Mahdi ﵇ will kill the *dajjal* at Bab al-Ludd.

Other signs of the third period include the appearance of Yajuj and Majuj (Gog and Magog) and the abandonment and depopulation of Madinah Tayyibah. This will occur forty years before the day of Standing.

Then all that will remain will be a city of date palms. This indicates towards the nature of the age in which Imam Mahdi عليه السلام will appear.

The destruction of the Ka'bah and the rising of the sun from the West are also from among the twelve signs of the end of time.

The Ahadith also report the appearance of the *Dabbatul 'l-Ard* (the Beast of the earth) who will populate the entire world and be similar in form to the dinosaurs.

The entire world will be engulfed by smoke (*Dukhan*) for forty days, the Qur'an will be taken up into the heavens, people will open their masahif and the pages will be blank. Even the huffaz will no longer be able to recall its blessed verses.

There shall blow a breeze, bearing a pleasant scent, due to which all believers shall be caused to die and only disbelievers and sinners will remain alive.

Finally a fire will start from Hadramawt in Yemen, that shall gather all the people in the world at the land of *Mahshar* and the events of the day of *Qiyamah* will begin.

These are the twelve Major Signs of the End of Time; beginning with the appearance of Imam Muhammad al-Mahdi عليه السلام.

CHAPTER SIX
PERSONALITY OF IMAM MAHDI عليه السلام

What follows is a brief introduction to Imam Muhammad Mahdi's ﷺ personality, which will be discussed later in the light of relevant traditions.

Muhammad ibn Abdullah al-Alawi, al-Hasani, al-Husayni, al-Fatimi, al-Hashimi will be born in Madinah Tayyibah to a mother from the lineage of Imam Hasan ؓ and a father from the lineage of Imam Husayn ؓ.

As pointed out earlier, there is a difference between the teachings of the Ahlu's-Sunnah and those of the Shi'ite community regarding the birth of Imam Mahdi ﷺ. The Shi'ites believe that he was born as the son of Imam Hasan al-Askari, the 12th Imam, and when he was four or eight years old he disappeared into a cave and will appear again. Hence they give him the title of Imam *Ghayb*, the hidden Imam, and Imam az-Zaman. Both the Ahlu's-Sunnah and the Shiites give the title, Imam Muntadhar (the awaited Imam) to him, because he is awaited by the whole *ummah*. Whoever is not waiting for him is lacking in faith.

He will be forty years old when he receives the *ba'yah* - oath of allegiance, although according to some traditions, he will be between thirty and forty at that time. His first *ba'yah* is also referred to as his 'appearance'. He will receive *ba'yah* for the first time at the Ka'abah between the Black Stone and the Station of Ibrahim. The first people to give their oath of allegiance to him will be the seven leading scholars of the world, who will have come from all over the world. Then three hundred and thirteen high-ranking soldiers, the same number as the *As'habu'l-Badr*, will take his hand in an oath of allegiance. Then the senior *awliyah* of Iraq and the *abdal* of Greater Syria will come and take his hand.

There are many ahadith regarding his physical appearance and detailed descriptions of his physical qualities.

His face will be handsome, with a broad forehead accompanied with large black eyes and a prominent nose. He will have a fair complexion tinted with red and will have a black mole on his right cheek and his face will radiate like a shining star. He will have a gap between his front teeth from which light will emanate. He will have a thick black beard and long black hair that will curl beneath the ears.

The mark of the Prophet ﷺ – *alamatu'n-nabi* – will be stamped between his shoulder blades.

He will wear a turban on his head. Interestingly enough, at this point in time, no one in Makkah or Madinah wears the turban. The present trend is to wear a cloth with red embroidery on it, draped over the head. The culture and trend there has not yet changed back to wearing a turban.

Minor points like these need to be analysed and understood in light of our subject, which is to determine the time when Imam Muhammad Mahdi عليه السلام is due to appear.

His character will be Arab but his physical appearance will seem to be non-Arab, meaning that his personality will be a mixture of the main features of both Arabs and non-Arabs. This is pointing to the fact that he will be an international personality, being the Caliph of the whole *ummah* and Allah's last caliph and imam for the entire world. Three thousand angels will always travel with him, as a part of his army. He will live for forty years after the *ba'yah.*

There are different narrations about the duration of his khilafah and rule; seven years, nine years, twenty years, thirty years, forty years and forty-nine years are all mentioned. These narrations will be discussed later when the duration of his rule will be derived from them. Nevertheless what is clear is that he is going to live for forty years after the *ba'yah.* His rule will span the whole globe. The details of all the areas that he will conquer will be given later, as the Prophet ﷺ gave a detailed account of all of this. The capital of his global state will be Jerusalem – *Baitu'l-Maqdis.* He will rule from Jerusalem for fourteen years.

Imam Nu'aym ibn Hammad narrated from Sayyidina Ali رضي الله عنه that the Prophet ﷺ said:

> *'Imam Mahdi عليه السلام will be born in Madinah. He will be from the Ahlu'l-Bayt. His name will be the same as mine. He will make hijrah to Jerusalem. His beard will be thick. His eyes will seem as though they have kohl on. His teeth will be shining and have gaps between them. He will have a mole on his cheek. He will wear a woollen cloak. He will have the sword of the Prophet ﷺ in his hand. He will wear the cloak of the Prophet ﷺ. He will have the assistance of three thousand angels.'*

CHAPTER SEVEN
QUR'ANIC REFERENCE TO THE VICOTORY OF IMAM MAHDI عليه السلام

وَقَضَيْنَا إِلَى بَنِي إِسْرَائِيلَ فِي الْكِتَابِ لَتُفْسِدُنَّ فِي الْأَرْضِ مَرَّتَيْنِ وَلَتَعْلُنَّ
عُلُوًّا كَبِيرًا ۝ فَإِذَا جَاءَ وَعْدُ أُولَاهُمَا بَعَثْنَا عَلَيْكُمْ عِبَادًا لَّنَا أُولِي بَأْسٍ شَدِيدٍ
فَجَاسُوا خِلَالَ الدِّيَارِ وَكَانَ وَعْدًا مَّفْعُولًا ۝ ثُمَّ رَدَدْنَا لَكُمُ الْكَرَّةَ عَلَيْهِمْ
وَأَمْدَدْنَاكُم بِأَمْوَالٍ وَبَنِينَ وَجَعَلْنَاكُمْ أَكْثَرَ نَفِيرًا ۝ إِنْ أَحْسَنتُمْ أَحْسَنتُمْ
لِأَنفُسِكُمْ وَإِنْ أَسَأْتُمْ فَلَهَا فَإِذَا جَاءَ وَعْدُ الْآخِرَةِ لِيَسُوؤُوا وُجُوهَكُمْ
وَلِيَدْخُلُوا الْمَسْجِدَ كَمَا دَخَلُوهُ أَوَّلَ مَرَّةٍ وَلِيُتَبِّرُوا مَا عَلَوْا تَتْبِيرًا ۝

"And in the Book We categorically conveyed to the Children of Israel: 'You shall twice make mischief and behave very aggressively against the obedience to Allah ﷻ. So when the promised first time of the two came We sent against you those of Our servants to subdue you who were strong and powerful warriors. Then they chased (searching for) you into your dwellings. And (it) was a promise to be fulfilled. Then We turned the dominance for you over them to your favour and helped you by (affluence in) wealth and children thus adding to your numerical strength. If you do good, you do it (only) for your own benefit but if you do evil, you shall sin against your own souls. Then, when the second promised time came (We sent against you other tyrants) so that, (lashing and whipping), they should mutilate your faces and enter the al-Aqsa Mosque (the same way) as the (invaders) had entered it the first time and (this was also

In these verses Allah ﷻ talks about the Banu Isra'il, the Israelites, and Jerusalem, al-Quds. He ﷻ mentions *Baitu'l-Maqdis*, the continual attacks on it and it being conquered. People being dominant and then others being dominated; so the attacks and dominations of various times are mentioned.

Commentators on the Holy Qur'an have made different interpretations of the second event referred to in these *ayats*. Some have linked it to the past and some to the future. If it is a matter of the past then the meaning would be: "When the time for the second event came then others were made to rule over you." If it is about future events then the meaning would be: "When the time of the second event comes then others will be made to rule over you. They will beat you so much due to your treachery that your faces will be disfigured. So that they enter Masjidu'l-Aqsa, just like they entered it the first time they attacked and conquered it, so that they destroy the place that they have conquered and dominated," in other words so that they totally dominate you and make you powerless.

The *mufassirin* have interpreted verse number seven in many ways.

Such topics in the Holy Qur'an are known as Qur'anic predictions. Qur'anic predictions are a subdivision among the various sciences of the Holy Qur'an. There are many predictions

[1] Qur'an (Bani Israel), 17: 4-7

made in the Holy Qur'an regarding what is going to happen in the future, just as the Holy Qur'an also discusses the stories of past nations. This verse is either referring to events undergone by a past nation or is foretelling future events.

The *imams* of *tafsir* have taken account of the comments made by the *Sahabah* and *Tabi'un* with reference to various Qur'anic passages and on that basis have made various predictions and interpretations, which they discuss in their *tafseers.*

None of the interpretations of this verse have been declared to be incorrect. One of those interpretations was that of Imam Ibn Jarir at-Tabari in his *tafsir*, *Jami'u'l-Bayan*, also known as *Tafsir at-Tabari.* This narration is from the Companion, Hudhayfah ibn al-Yaman', mentioning its original application. Imam Jalalu'd-din as-Suyuti also has this narration in his *tafsir, ad-Durru'l-Manthur.* Imam as-Suyuti takes this narration as a hadith, with the Companion narrating the words of the Prophet ﷺ.

The narration is that the Holy Prophet ﷺ said that this verse – that they will be conquered and dominated by others who will beat them so much that their faces will be disfigured– is referring to the time of Imam Muhammad Mahdi عليه السلام, indicating that Imam Muhammad Mahdi عليه السلام will again conquer and enter Jerusalem and that he will return the city to its past honour and grandeur. He will also return to it its treasures, which were looted in a previous age. The narration further states that in this victory and conquest of Jerusalem, which will take place under the leadership of Imam Muhammad Mahdi عليه السلام, his army will use seventeen hundred warships.

قَالَ رَسُولُ اللهِ صَلَّى اللَّهُ عَلَيْهِ وَآلِهِ وَسَلَّمَ: فَهَذَا مِنْ صِفَةِ حُلِّيِّ بَيتِ الْمَقْدِسِ وَيَرُدُّهُ الْمَهْدِيُّ إِلَى بَيْتِ الْمَقْدِسِ، وَهُوَ أَلْفُ سَفِينَةٍ وَسَبْعُمِائَةِ سَفِينَةٍ يُرْسَى بِهَا عَلَى يَافَا، حَتَّى تَنْتَقِلَ إِلَى بَيْتِ الْمَقْدِسِ. وَبِهَا يَجْتَمِعُ إِلَيْهِ الأَوَّلُونَ وَالآخِرُونَ۔

"The Holy Prophet ﷺ said, "This is the description of the jewels of Bait al-Maqdis and Imam Mahdi will return it to Bait al-Maqdis and it consists of one thousand ships and seven hundred ships out of which, one thousand will be anchored on YAFA then these jewels will be returned to Bait al-Maqdis; a place where the first (early) ones and the last (later) ones will get together."[2]

This is a crucial point in the context of the time when Imam Muhammad Mahdi (a.s.) will appear. The word used here is *safinah* – warship – and not *fulk* – boat. So these are not seventeen hundred ordinary boats or ships but seventeen hundred warships. Then the narration goes onto say that all early and later nations and tribes will be gathered at Jerusalem, which gives us another point worthy of attention.

Imam Muhammad Mahdi (a.s.) will conquer Jerusalem for the last time. He will make it the global capital of his global state, his global caliphate. As we have seen there are different narrations

---

[2] Tabari, Jami'-ul-bayan fi tafsir-il-Qur'an, vol. 15, p. 22
Qurtubi, al-Jami' li-ahkam-il-Qur'an, vol. 10, pp. 222, 223.
Suyuti, ad-Durr-ul-Manthur fit-tafsir bil-ma'thur, vol. 5, p. 243.

regarding the total period of his rule. The more reliable narrations state the period to be from seven to nine to twenty years, although there are narrations that mention a longer period. Taking the more reliable narrations, it seems as though he will rule for twenty years. Out of that period seven or nine years will be the period during which he will have the status of *Khalifatu'llah ala'l-ard*, in other words rule over the whole earth. That global state will be the biggest global empire ever seen and Islam will then be the supreme power in the world.

Islamic governance in the form of the *khilafah* of Allah ﷻ and *khilafah* of the Prophet ﷺ will rule over every part of the globe. Before this period his rule will cover the Arabian Peninsula, Greater Syria, Constantinople, Europe and some other regions for about thirteen years. Other states such as those in the Far East and South East Asia will be conquered later.

Imam Mahdi's victory – not a supernatural event

At this point it is worth mentioning those people and their gullible friends who have announced that Imam Muhammad Mahdi عليه السلام has already been born and will appear in the next few years. These views have been published in newspapers and have been widely publicised. Many Arab and non-Arab scholars have supported and spread such views. There are scholars who have been performing the Hajj every year for several years now, so that they may be among those who take direct *ba'yah* with Imam Muhammad Mahdi عليه السلام. Some say that he was born in 1960 and will announce his appearance any year now.

The point to ponder on is that if the time of his appearance is imminent then the events on the ground need to reflect that. Neither the appearance of the Imam nor his governance across the globe is a supernatural affair.

Contra distinctly, the rule of the Imam will be established as a result of natural process: whereby the circumstances will gradually alter to suit his arrival.

The claim that the Imam Mahdi عليه السلام will appear in Makkah and within a matter of two to three years develop and establish a global empire is no more than a fallacy.

Analysis of current information provides ample contextual evidence that for a Muslim leader to establish global rule within the next two to three years is far from possible.

Furthermore the Muslim ummah does not possess the seventeen hundred warships, referred to in the previous section. The historical process of the rise and fall of nations and powers will continue for a period of time yet.

A study of the abundant ahadith on this subject, demonstrate that the current global superpower may not remain. By the time Imam Mahdi عليه السلام appears the balance of power could very well have shifted.

In fact, the prophetic traditions allude to the supremacy of power resting in Europe.

This all cumulatively illustrates that the geopolitical circumstances of the Muslims do not logically permit the appearance of Imam Mahdi عليه السلام.

CHAPTER EIGHT

EVENTS AT THE TIME OF IMAM MAHDI عليه السلام

Appearance of Imam Muhammad Mahdi عليه السلام

Imam Muhammad Mahdi عليه السلام will be born in an area around Madinah Munawwarah called Qar'ah. According to the traditions he will live there for about thirty to forty years. He will then receive *ba'yah* in Makkah at the time of Hajj, between the Black Stone and the Station of Ibrahim. Initially three hundred and thirteen senior members of the *ummah* will take an oath of allegiance at his hand, followed by seven senior scholars of the *ummah*. Later when Jerusalem is conquered, he will migrate there and establish it as the capital of the Islamic state.

There will be many disruptions and tribulations before his birth including many earthquakes.

Imam Mahdi عليه السلام shall be the greatest of a long line of revivers (Mujaddidin), the greatest chieftain and leader of mankind. He shall occupy the highest spiritual rank ever possessed by any one individual (*wilayah al-udhmah*). He will be the last and most eminent of the Ummah of the Prophet Muhammad ﷺ.

عن أم سلمة قالت: سمعت رسول الله صلى الله عليه وآله وسلم يقول: سيكون بعدي خسف بالمشرق وخسف بالمغرب في جزيرة العرب. قلت: يا رسول الله! أيخسف بالأرض وفيها الصالحون؟ قال لها رسول الله صلى الله عليه وآله وسلم: نعم، إذا أكثر أهلها الخبث.

"Umm Salama narrated: she said: I heard the Holy Prophet ﷺ say, "After me, there will be sinking of the people into the earth in the East and sinking of the people into the earth in the West within the Arabian Peninsula." I said: O messenger of Allah! Will the earth swallow people while there are pious amongst them? The Holy Prophet ﷺ said to her, "Yes, it will occur while its inhabitants are more involved in evil."[1]

The Appearance of Dajjal

Due to partial study of the vast corpus of hadith literature many individuals have asserted that the *Dajjal* is not an individual who shall appear before the End of Time, but rather is a philosophy or a socio-political system. This however is untrue.

There are undoubtedly 'dajjalic' powers and systems that are paving the way for the *Dajjals* appearance. Similarly there are powers of a 'Mahdi' nature that strive to disseminate the richness of the Muslim tradition.

The Dajjal will have an army of seventy thousand Jews. He will wear clothing made from a material called 'Dabees'. He will emerge from a place called *Yahudiyyah* between Greater Syria and Iraq.

He will resemble in appearance to a person called Abdul Uzzah

[1] Tabarani, al-Mu'jam-ul-awsat, vol. 4, p. 74 # 3647.
Haythami related it in Majma'-uz-zawai'd, vol. 8, p. 11, and said, Tabarani narrated it and its men are thiqa (trustworthy).

who lived at the time of the Holy Prophet ﷺ. The colour of his hair will be brown and his hair will be curly. He will be blind from his left eye and his right eye will be disfigured.

The word '*kafir*' will be written on his forehead. The three letters *kaf - fa - ra* will be written separately. Everybody, whether literate or illiterate, will be able to read them. The vehicle upon which he will travel is referred to by the word '*himar*' and most translators have translated it as 'donkey'. The word '*himar*' is being used symbolically, as that time will not be the time of travelling on donkeys because it will not be possible to travel around the whole globe on a donkey.

Describing the craft that the Dajjal will be travelling on, the Holy Prophet ﷺ said that its two ears will be forty hand spans apart that is forty multiplied by nine inches, which comes to approximately thirty feet. Here the word 'ears' in fact refers to wings, which indicates an aeroplane. The reason the word donkey was used is because its ears point upwards while the ears of other animals, such as elephants, point downwards. This seems to be an indication of the high-speed aircraft of that time, which the Dajjal will use when travelling.

The Dajjal will firstly make a claim to Prophethood and then claim to be God. He will travel all over the world causing chaos and carnage everywhere except for Makkah, Madinah and Jerusalem. He will stay outside the boundaries of these cities. At that time there will be seven gates outside the two cities of Makkah and Madinah and there will be walls around them. There will be an angel at each gate and Dajjal will be specifically banned from entering Makkah and Madinah. All hypocrites living in Makkah and Madinah at that time will be evicted. They will all accept the call of Dajjal and go and join his army. Only believers will remain and they will be on the side of Imam Muhammad Mahdi عليه السلام.

The majority of Jews will be on the side of Dajjal, with him having an army of seventy thousand Jews.

Arrival and description of Prophet Isa عليه السلام

The third personality will be Prophet Isa عليه السلام. He will descend from the heavens during night, either on the eastern minaret of Masjid Umawi in Damascus or in Jerusalem.

The Prophet ﷺ is reported to have said that the physical appearance of Prophet Isa will be the same as that of Urwa ibn Mas'ud رضي الله عنه, one of his Companions. He will be of medium height, fair skinned with a tinge of redness. His hair will be straight with no curls and will be shoulder length.

Initially the most pious of people, consisting of eight hundred men and four hundred women will join him.

The Prophet Isa عليه السلام will descend at the time of *Fajr* after *Iqamah* has been recited and Imam Mahdi عليه السلام has occupied the Imams prayer mat.

Upon seeing the Prophet Isa عليه السلام Imam Mahdi عليه السلام shall withdraw and attempt to join the congregation but will be told by Prophet Isa عليه السلام that '*the Imam of the Ummah, shall lead the ummah in prayer*'.

This event alone is an adequate presentation of the lofty status of the Imam and hence those who wish to demean and desecrate his holy being, must repent and ratify to the creed of the majority of our Ulema.

As for those who wholly reject the appearance of the Imam the Ulema have differed.

The predominant position of the Ulema of Sunna wal Jama'ah is that it amounts to *Fisq* and not *kufr* (disbelief).

Nonetheless the Ulema unanimously concur that it constitutes misguidance and error.

Once the prayer is completed Imam Mahdi ﷺ and Prophet Isa ﷺ along with an army of Muslims shall battle the Anti-Christ and his army comprising of 70,000 people.

The Dajjal will be killed at *Bab-al Lud* in Palestine (as transmitted in the Prophetic tradition). Known as Lod, this exact location exists inside Israel Frontiers as an airport.

The precision and authenticity of the Prophets information is yet another manifestation of the vastness of knowledge He ﷺ has been blessed with.

Signs and Events before the coming of Imam Muhammad Mahdi ﷺ

As previously mentioned the coming of Imam Mahdi ﷺ will be indicated by the occurrence of three major earthquakes, causing unimaginable destruction.

Before his coming the sun will rise from the west, accompanied by a comet with a very long tail, which will be seen towards the

East. It will be very bright and will be seen for a long time. In the first Ramadan after that, there will be a solar eclipse on the first of the month and there will also be two lunar eclipses during it.

In the year that Imam Muhammad Mahdi عليه السلام reveals himself there shall be a battle at Mina during the Hajj. The battle will be between tribes, resulting in great destruction and bloodshed on a very large scale.

Events at the time of Imam Mahdi's appearance

Imam Mahdi's عليه السلام appearance will result in a series of battles and victories, bringing the whole of the Arab world under his rule.

One such battle will rage between Imam Mahdi عليه السلام and a man called Sufyani, who will be from the tribe of Yazeed and will emerge from Greater Syria. He will cause great bloodshed, killing thousands of people in Kufa and other cities of Iraq.

عَنْ أَبِي هُرَيْرَةَ قَالَ: قَالَ رَسُولُ اللَّهِ صَلَّى اللَّهُ عَلَيْهِ وَآلِهِ وَسَلَّمَ: تَخْرُجُ مِنْ خُرَاسَانَ رَايَاتٌ سُودٌ لَا يَرُدُّهَا شَيْءٌ حَتَّى تُنْصَبَ بِإِيلِيَاءَ.

"Abu Hurayrah narrates that the Holy Prophet ﷺ said, "(Armies with) black flags will appear from Khurasaan, no power will be able to stop them until they (those flags) are finally erected in Eelia' (Baitul Maqdas)."[2]

[2] Tirmidhi, *as-Sunan*, vol. 4, p. 531 # 2269.
Ahmad bin Hambal, *al-Musnad*, vol. 2, p. 365, # 8760.

The death and destruction caused by Sufyani will be avenged by a group of people from Kufa and Khurasan. The word Khurasan is clearly mentioned in traditions, as is the word Kufa. One of the notable descriptions of this army will be that they will fly black flags like the Armies of the Prophet ﷺ used to and they will be led by a man from the Tamimi clan called Shu'aib ibn Salih at-Tamimi.

Numerous traditions from the *sihah sitta* report that Sufyani and his army will head towards Makkah upon hearing about Imam Mahdi ﷺ but they will be destroyed before reaching their destination, at a place called Baida'a. Recognising this as one of the signs of the appearance of Imam Mahdi ﷺ many armies from around the world will be mobilised, including the army of Shu'aib ibn Salih at-Tamimi as well as the army of a man called Hashimi.

Some prophetic traditions state that he (Hashimi) will be Imam Mahdi's half brother, in that they will have the same father but not the same mother.

Together the armies of Shu'aib ibn Salih at-Tamimi and Hashimi will report to Imam Muhammad Mahdi ﷺ. So all these armies will unite together as one huge force under the command of Imam Muhammad Mahdi ﷺ and move towards Greater Syria and Istanbul.

The advancement of Imam Mahdi's army away from the Arabian Peninsula into the rest of the world will lead to the

---

Tabarani, *al-Mu'jam-ul-awsat*, vol. 4, p. 31 # 3536.

creation of a global Islamic state.

The geopolitical map of the world will be considerably different at that time where Istanbul will be the capital of Europe hence Turkey will not be under Muslim rule.

The Prophet ﷺ also said that there will be a battle against the Turks resulting in Turkey being conquered.

The largest barracks of Imam Muhammad Mahdi's عليه السلام army will be in Greater Syria so support will also come to the armies from within that area. After conquering Istanbul, Imam Muhammad Mahdi عليه السلام will conquer Jerusalem, which will be made the capital of the global Islamic State and this will be followed by the conquest of Rome.

The conquest of Istanbul and Rome indicates that the major and strongest part of Europe will be overcome. Then Imam Mahdi عليه السلام will send his armies to conquer the Indian sub-continent.

Another major event to occur at the time of Imam Mahdi's appearance is the gathering of forty *abdal* from Greater Syria. The forty *abdal* and the *awliya* of Iraq will come to Makkah and make *ba'yah* at the hand of Imam Muhammad Mahdi عليه السلام.

Traditions about events at the time of Imam Mahdi عليه السلام

In discussing the subject of Imam Mahdi, greater emphasis has been laid upon traditions from the *Sihah Sitta.*

However, other of books of traditions by various Imams also give a detailed account of the events of the end of time, namely of the time of Imam Mahdi عليه السلام.

The Holy Prophet ﷺ is reported to have said that there will be a battle of Hind (India). The battle of India referred to here cannot be that of Muhammad ibn Qasim or that of Sultan Mahmud Ghaznavi. The reason being that the majority of hadith books mention this tradition under the chapter of *fitan* and under the signs of *Qiyamah*, although an-Nasa'i did mention this tradition in the book of Jihad. It is also mentioned together with the traditions concerning Imam Muhammad Mahdi عليه السلام and Prophet Isa عليه السلام. This establishes the fact that this tradition is not referring to the two earlier advances on India.

عَنْ أَبِي هُرَيْرَةَ قَالَ: وَعَدَنَا رَسُولُ اللّٰهِ صَلَّى اللّٰهُ عَلَيْهِ وَآلِهِ وَسَلَّمَ غَزْوَةَ الْهِنْدِ، فَإِنْ أَدْرَكْتُهَا أُنْفِقْ فِيهَا نَفْسِي وَمَالِي، فَإِنْ أُقْتَلْ كُنْتُ مِنْ أَفْضَلِ الشُّهَدَاءِ، وَإِنْ أَرْجِعْ فَأَنَا أَبُو هُرَيْرَةَ الْمُحَرَّرُ۔

"Narrated by Abu Hurayrah. He said: the Holy Prophet ﷺ promised us a war with India. If I was to witness that war, I will sacrifice (literally spend) myself and my property. If I were killed, I will be amongst the best martyrs, and if I was to return then I will be Abu Huraira, the freed one (from the fire of Hell)."[3]

---

[3] Related by Nasa'i and its chain of transmission is fair (*isnaduhu hasan*).
Nasa'i, *as-Sunan*, vol. 6, p. 42, # 3173, 3174.
Nasa'i, *as-Sunan al-kubra*, vol. 3, p. 28, # 4382, 4383.
Ibn Abi 'Asim, *Kitab-ul-Jihad*, vol. 2, p. 669 # 291.
Ibn Mansur, *as-Sunan*, vol. 2, p. 178 # 2375.
Bayhaqi, *as-Sunan al-kubra*, vol. 9, p. 176 # 18380.

It is narrated by Abu Hurayrah ؓ that the Prophet ﷺ told them about the Battle of Hind. He ﷺ said that if he was alive for the battle then he would spend himself and his resources on it, and if he were martyred in it then he would be among the greatest of martyrs. Those who survive the battle will be saved from Hellfire. In other narrations the words that are used are proof that this refers to a battle at the time of Imam Muhammad Mahdi ؑ.

عَنْ ثَوْبَانَ, مَوْلَى رَسُولِ اللّٰهِ صَلَّى اللّٰهُ عَلَيْهِ وَآلِهِ وَسَلَّمَ, قَالَ: قَالَ رَسُولُ اللّٰهِ
صَلَّى اللّٰهُ عَلَيْهِ وَآلِهِ وَسَلَّمَ: عِصَابَتَانِ مِنْ أُمَّتِي أَحْرَزَهُمَا اللّٰهُ مِنَ النَّارِ:
عِصَابَةٌ تَغْزُو الْهِنْدَ, وَعِصَابَةٌ تَكُونُ مَعَ عِيسَى ابْنِ مَرْيَمَ عَلَيْهِمَا السَّلَامُ۔

"Thawban, the freed-slave of the Holy Prophet ﷺ, narrates that Holy Prophet ﷺ said, "There will be two groups from my Ummah - Allah ﷻ has saved them from the fire of hell; the group that will invade India and the one that will be with 'Isa bin Maryam (accompanies him and support him)."[4]

Based on the above tradition it has been construed that these two armies will be in battle simultaneously as Prophet Isa ؑ will not

---

[4] Related by Nasa'i and Ahmad and its men are *thiqa* (trustworthy).
Nasa'i, *as-Sunan*, vol. 6, p. 42, # 3175.
Nasa'i, *as-Sunan al-kubra*, vol. 3, p. 28, # 4384.
Ahmad bin Hambal, *al-Musnad*, vol. 5, p. 278.
Bukhari, *at-Tarikh al-Kabir*, vol. 6, p. 72 # 1747.
Bayhaqi, *as-Sunan al-kubra*, vol. 9, p. 176 # 18381.
Tabarani, *al-Mu'jam al-awsat*, vol. 6, p. 24 # 6741.

go to India but instead Imam Muhammad Mahdi عليه السلام will send an army to the whole of South East Asia and it will be conquered. The leaders of India will be arrested and brought before Imam Muhammad Mahdi عليه السلام.

Furthermore, Imam an-Nasa'i transmits traditions about the battle of the Turks and the Battle of Abyssinia, which will also take place at the time of Imam Muhammad Mahdi عليه السلام, indicating that all traditions are related to the same time period.

Imam Ibn Kathir compiled a book entitled *an-Nihaya fi'l-Fitani wal Malahim*, in relevance to the *fitan* that shall take place as signs of the Last hour and the events surrounding Imam Muhammad Mahdi عليه السلام and Prophet Isa عليه السلام. In this book Imam Ibn Kathir mentions the battles of Hind and Sind under the chapters about signs of the nearness of *Qiyamah*.

In the *Musnad* of Imam Ahmad ibn Hanbal, Abu Hurariah رضي الله عنه states that the Prophet ﷺ said that armies would be sent to Sind and Hind. The word *ba'ath* is used indicating that Imam Muhammad Mahdi عليه السلام will not go himself but will deploy his armies.

Abu Hurayrah رضي الله عنه narrates that the Prophet ﷺ said: "In my Ummah an army will be sent towards Sind and Hind who will conquer Sind (Pakistan) and Hind (India)."

If one was to ponder on these traditions with regards to proclamations made by certain people about the appearance of Imam Mahdi عليه السلام one would realise that such announcements are groundless. The balance of power in the world has not changed and neither is the conquest of India in sight, in fact she is becoming a super power as is China.

عَنْ أَبِي هُرَيْرَةَ قَالَ: قَالَ رَسُولُ اللّٰهِ صَلَّى اللّٰهُ عَلَيْهِ وَآلِهِ وَسَلَّمَ: تَخْرُجُ مِنْ خُرَاسَانَ رَايَاتٌ سُودٌ لَا يَرُدُّهَا شَيْءٌ حَتَّى تُنْصَبَ بِإِيلِيَاءَ.

"Abu Hurayrah narrates that the Holy Prophet ﷺ said, "(Armies with) black flags will appear from Khurasaan, no power will be able to stop them untill they (those flags) are finally erected in Eelia' (Baitul Maqdas)."[5]

In the *Musnad* of Ahmad ibn Hanbal, Abu Hurayrah ؓ narrates that the Prophet ﷺ said that armies carrying black flags will come from Khurasan. Nothing will be able to stop them. They will advance to Jerusalem and raise their flag there. Then the conquest of China is mentioned. Imam Ibn Hajar al-Makki has mentioned in his book *al-Qawl al-Mukhtasar* that China will also be conquered at the time of these battles.

At-Tirmidhi relates that the Prophet ﷺ said that in the Greatest War six hundred thousand people will be killed. The first battle will be in Constantinople, which the Muslims will fight in the absence of Imam Mahdi ؑ, in this battle forty thousand people will be killed.

As that war reaches a successful climax, a false rumour of the

[5] Tidmidhi, *as-Sunan*, vol. 4, p. 531 # 2269.
Ahmad bin Hambal, *al-Musnad*, vol. 2, p. 365, # 8760.
Tabarani, *al-Mu'jam-ul-awsat*, vol. 4, p. 31 # 3536.

appearance of Dajjal shall spread. As a result of this the army will return from Constantinople to join Imam Mahdi ﷺ, in order to reinforce him and they will not be able to finish their task.

Imam Muhammad Mahdi ﷺ together with all his armies from Makkah, Madinah and Greater Syria, will advance towards Greater Syria and Rome and finally to Constantinople again with an army of seventy thousand men.

In the second attack on Constantinople by Imam Mahdi ﷺ and his army she will be aided from both the East and West.

All the armies from countries around the world will come to save Jerusalem, Constantinople and Rome.

After conquering Constantinople Imam Muhammad Mahdi ﷺ will send armies to the countries that sent forces to fight against his, forces resulting in the conquest of China and India. Six hundred thousand people will be killed in this Great War and it will result in a victory for Imam Mahdi ﷺ.

The great danger of 'Mahdi mongering'

In the process of calculating the time for the appearance of Imam Muhammad Mahdi ﷺ, the circumstances mentioned in these traditions from *Sihah Sittah* cannot be ignored. In order to determine the correct time for the coming of Imam Muhammad Mahdi ﷺ, all of the relevant traditions must be consulted as a whole and the circumstances at that time must be taken into account. The geopolitical situation of the whole area at that time must be carefully considered. Only in the light of all this information, can any realistic estimate be possible.

For this reason it is necessary to be very cautious when making assumptions based on certain current events and circumstances.

There are many traditions, which are very detailed in their explanation regarding the signs and events of the end of time. By the means of a thorough analysis and extensive study of these traditions one can visualise the circumstances in which the above-mentioned events will take place.

Great changes have yet to take place. The state of the *ummah* at that time will be such that Imam Muhammad Mahdi عليه السلام will be able to send armies to Constantinople, Rome, Europe, India, China and at the same time rule over the Arab world with Greater Syria also under his control, prior to establishing a global empire. All of this will only happen when the global situation corresponds to this picture and is leading in this direction.

The strength and power of Imam Muhammad Mahdi's عليه السلام army can be ascertained from the fact that when he goes to conquer Jerusalem he will be using one thousand seven hundred warships, as mentioned earlier. He will be the leader of the world's greatest super power at that time. In Sunan Abu Dawud, this tradition is under the heading: *al-malhamatu'l-kubra.* In Sunan Abu Dawud the book of *fitan* has a chapter on Imam Muhammad Mahdi عليه السلام mentioning the circumstances, events and the battles at that time.

عَنْ مُعَاذِ بْنِ جَبَلٍ، عَنِ النَّبِيِّ صَلَّى اللهُ عَلَيْهِ وَآلِهِ وَسَلَّمَ قَالَ: الْمَلْحَمَةُ الْعُظْمَى وَفَتْحُ الْقُسْطَنْطِينِيَّةِ وَخُرُوجُ الدَّجَّالِ فِي سَبْعَةِ أَشْهُرٍ.

"Mu'adh ibn Jabal ﷺ reports that the Holy Prophet ﷺ said: "The greatest war, the conquest of Constantinople and the coming forth of the Dajjal (Antichrist - literally the impostor) will take place within a period of seven months."[6]

This point is worthy of deliberation, for it gives a clear cut time scale to the Great War under the leadership of Imam Muhammad Mahdi ﷺ, the conquest of Constantinople and the appearance of Dajjal.

In the following tradition in *Sunan Abi Dawud*, Abdullah ibn Busr relates that the Prophet ﷺ said that there would be a period of six years between the start of the Great War and the conquest of Constantinople, indicating that the Great War will continue for six years.

---

[6] Tirmidhi graded it *hasan* (fair) in *al-Jami'us-Sahih*, vol. 4, p. 509 # 2238.
Abu Dawud, *as-Sunan*, vol. 4, p. 110 # 4295.
Ibn Majah, *as-Sunan*, vol. 2, p. 1370 # 4092.
Ahmad bin Hambal, *al-Musnad*, vol. 5, p. 234 # 22098.
Hakim, *al-Mustadrak*, vol. 4, vol. 473 # 8313.
Tabarani, *al-Mu'jam-ul-kabir*, vol. 20, p. 91 # 173, 174.
Nu'aym bin Hammad, *al-Fitn*, vol. 2, p. 524 # 1474.

عَنْ عَبْدِ اللّٰهِ بْنِ بُسْرٍ، أَنَّ رَسُولَ اللّٰهِ صَلَّى اللّٰهُ عَلَيْهِ وَآلِهِ وَسَلَّمَ قَالَ: بَيْنَ الْمَلْحَمَةِ وَفَتْحِ الْمَدِينَةِ سِتُّ سِنِينَ، وَيَخْرُجُ الْمَسِيحُ الدَّجَّالُ فِي السَّابِعَةِ. وَقَالَ أَبُو دَاوُد: هٰذَا أَصَحُّ مِنْ حَدِيثِ عِيسَى.

"Abdullah ibn Busr narrates that the Holy Prophet ﷺ said: "The time between the great war and the conquest of the city (Constantinople) will be six years, and the Dajjal (Antichris – literally the impostor) will appear in the seventh (year)." And Abu Dawud said, "This tradition is more authentic than the one related by Tirmidhi."[7]

In some traditions it is related that a period of six years will elapse from the time in which Imam Mahdi (عليه السلام) appears to the conquest of Jerusalem.

The Prophet ﷺ is also reported to have said that in the seventh year the Dajjal will appear.

Imam Muhammad Mahdi (عليه السلام) will have been ruling from Jerusalem for one year when Dajjal appears. Imam Abu Dawud also has a chapter entitled 'Jihad with the Turks' followed by traditions mentioning Basra and then the river Euphrates in Iraq, and that gold and oil will be discovered there.

---

[7] Abu Dawud, *as-Sunan*, vol. 4, p. 110 # 4296.
Ibn Majah, *as-Sunan*, vol. 2, p. 1370 # 4093.
Ahmad bin Hambal, *al-Musnad*, vol. 4, p. 189 # 17727.
Bazzar, *al-Musnad*, vol. 8, p. 431 # 3505.
Ibn Abi Shaybah, *al-Musnad*, vol. 7, p. 458 # 37208.

عَنْ أَبِي هُرَيْرَةَ قَالَ: قَالَ رَسُولُ اللهِ صَلَّى اللهُ عَلَيْهِ وَآلِهِ وَسَلَّمَ: لَوْ لَمْ يَبْقَ مِنَ الدُّنْيَا إِلَّا يَوْمٌ لَطَوَّلَهُ اللهُ عَزَّ وَجَلَّ حَتَّى يَمْلِكَ رَجُلٌ مِنْ أَهْلِ بَيْتِي، يَمْلِكُ جَبَلَ الدَّيْلَمِ وَالْقُسْطَنْطِينِيَّةَ.

Abu Huraira reports that the Messenger of Allah ﷺ said, "If only one day is left in this world, Allah the Almighty and Glorious will prolong it till a man of my family will take rule over Mount Dailam and Constantinople."[8]

In *Sunan Ibn Majah*, there is a hadith transmitted by Abu Hurayrah in which the Prophet ﷺ said, "Even if there is only one day left before *Qiyamah*, Allah ﷻ will prolong that day, as *Qiyamah* cannot come before the coming of my direct descendant from my Ahlu'l-Bait... He will conquer Constantinople and rule over it."

Once all four corners of the Earth have become part of the global Islamic State under the governance of Imam Mahdi ﷺ, he will reside in Jerusalem which will be the capital at the time, for fourteen years. He will be between thirty to forty years old and will live for a further forty years after his appearance in the Haram in Makkah. During this time Prophet Isa ﷺ will descend from the heavens.

---

[8] Ibn Majah, *as-Sunan*, vol. 2, p. 928 # 2779.
Ibn Ishaq, *Min hadith Khaythama*, vol. 1, p. 192.
Qazwini, *at-Tadwin fi akhbar Qazwin*, vol. 3, p. 297.
Daylamni, *Musnad al-Firdaws*, vol. 3, p. 372 # 5128 & vol. 5, p. 82 # 352.

So taking all the traditions together we can see that he will live for about eighty years altogether. Prophet Isa ﷺ will live for a further forty years after his descent and Dajjal will also live for forty years after his appearance.

Prophet Isa ﷺ will get married to a noble lady from the family of Prophet Ya'qub ﷺ and will have children. After taking part, and succeeding in all the challenges and battles he will encounter, he will go to *Haramayn Sharifayn* where he will perform Hajj and Umrah and then visit the Rawda of Mustafa ﷺ. He will greet the Prophet ﷺ and the Prophet ﷺ will reply to his greeting. Prophet Isa ﷺ will die there and will be buried besides Sayyidina Abu Bakr and Sayyidina Umar , in the company of the Prophet ﷺ.

At that time Africa will be a very big power. A king from Africa will govern continuously for twelve years. Then another ruler will replace him. After hearing of the great global state of Imam Muhammad Mahdi ﷺ, they will come and give their *ba'yah* of allegiance. Through this, Africa will become part of the global caliphate of Imam Muhammad Mahdi ﷺ. So the continents of Asia, Africa, Europe as well as the Arab World will be under his rule. This is the reason he will be known as the Caliph of God on earth.

After the passing away of Imam Muhammad Mahdi ﷺ, a man called al-Mansur will be appointed as the caliph to continue ruling the global Islamic state. His tenure will be twenty-one years. His rule will be followed by the rule of Hushaym al-Mahdi, his tenure will last for three years four months and ten days.

It is important to note that all these details are not available in any one book in this sequence and order. This information is a combination of various resources from numerous books of hadith. In collaborating the information one can envisage the sequence of events and accurately calculate the approximate time of the coming of Imam Muhammad Mahdi ﷺ. Reaching conclusions about such matters by referring to only one or two books inevitably results in misconceptions and grave errors.

CHAPTER NINE

TWELVE FINAL SIGNS OF THE NEARNESS OF QIYAMAH

During the course of this analysis, the twelve final signs that will take place very near to Qiyamah have been discussed in great detail. To review, the first sign is the appearance of Imam Muhammad Mahdi عليه السلام. The second is the appearance of Dajjal and the third is the descent of Prophet Isa عليه السلام from the heavens.

عَنْ أَبِي هُرَيْرَةَ رَضِيَ اللّٰهُ عَنْهُ، يَقُولُ: قَالَ رَسُولُ اللّٰهِ صَلَّى اللّٰهُ عَلَيْهِ وَآلِهِ وَسَلَّمَ: وَالَّذِي نَفْسِي بِيَدِهِ! لَيُوشِكَنَّ أَنْ يَنْزِلَ فِيكُمُ ابْنُ مَرْيَمَ حَكَمًا مُقْسِطًا، فَيَكْسِرَ الصَّلِيبَ، وَيَقْتُلَ الْخِنْزِيرَ، وَيَضَعَ الْجِزْيَةَ، وَيَفِيضَ الْمَالُ حَتَّى لَا يَقْبَلَهُ أَحَدٌ.

Abu Hurayrah narrates that the Messenger of Allah ﷺ said, "By Him in whose hands my soul rests! It is definitely close in time that Jesus عليه السلام, Son of Maryam (Mary) descends (or He is definitely about to descend) amongst you as a just ruler. He will break the cross, kill the swine and abolish jizya (a tax taken from the non-Muslims, against their protection by the Muslim government). And money will abound in such excess that no one will (wish to) accept it.[1]

[1] Bukhari, as-Sahih, vol. 2, pp. 774, 875 # 2109, 2344 & vol. 3, p. 1273 # 3264.
Muslim, as-Sahih, vol. 1. p. 135 # 155.
Tirmidhi, as-Sunan, vol. 4, p. 506 # 2233.
Nasa'i, as-Sunan, vol. 2, p. 1363 # 4087.

The fourth sign is the emergence of Yajuj and Majuj (Gog and Magog). They will be so great in number that they will dominate the whole world. The Holy Quran has mentioned this as:

حَتَّىٰٓ إِذَا فُتِحَتْ يَأْجُوجُ وَمَأْجُوجُ وَهُم مِّن كُلِّ حَدَبٍ يَنسِلُونَ

"Until when Gog and Magog are let loose and they will come down running from every high place."[2]

The fifth sign is the depopulation of Madinah. The reason for Madinah Tayyibah being depopulated is because people are mortal and will perish. Thus when it is the time for Madinah to be raised to the heavens, it will already be deserted. The people will have left during the time of Imam Muhammad Mahdi عليه السلام. The hypocrites will have left to join Dajjal and the believers will have gone to join Imam Muhammad Mahdi عليه السلام.

Madinah Tayyibah will be depopulated for forty years and the shape of the original Madinah that existed at the time of the Prophet ﷺ will again be visible. Spiritual intuition suggests that Allah ﷻ wishes to recreate the same Madinah that the Prophet ﷺ left behind – the city of date trees. He ﷻ will show the world, again, how the city of Madinah was when the Prophet ﷺ blessed it with his arrival.

Ahmad bin Hambal, al-Musnad, vol. 2, p. 240 # 7267.

[2] Qur'an (al-Ambiya'), 21: 96

The sixth sign is that the Ka'bah will be demolished. Rulers of Africa at that time will attack Makkah and destroy the Ka'bah.

عَنْ أَبِي هُرَيْرَةَ رَضِيَ اللهُ عَنْهُ، عَنِ النَّبِيِّ صَلَّى اللهُ عَلَيْهِ وَآلِهِ وَسَلَّمَ، قَالَ: يُخَرِّبُ الْكَعْبَةَ ذُو السُّوَيْقَتَيْنِ مِنَ الْحَبَشَةِ.

"Narrated Abu Hurayrah: The Prophet ﷺ said, "Dhus-Suwaiqa-tain (One with thin/short legs) from Ethiopia will demolish the Ka'ba."[3]

The traditions themselves do not give reasons for Madinah being depopulated and for the demolition of the Ka'bah, but the sayings of the *awliya* have been mentioned so that no misconceptions remain regarding why this should happen to such holy places. The task of *muhaditheen* is simply to record the traditions but Allah ﷻ has a channel of knowledge called *'ilm ladunni* which he transmits to his *awliya*. He ﷻ transfers knowledge from *al-mala'u'l-'ala* to His *awliya*.

Some *awliya, and 'urafa* (the saints of Allah) whose hearts are opened to such inspirations have explained that by depopulating Madinah and demolishing the Ka'bah, both of them will be raised

---

[3] Agreed upon by Bukhari and Muslim.
Bukhari, as-Sahih, vol. 2, pp. 578, 579 # 1514, 1519.
Muslim, as-Sahih, vol. 4, p. 2232 # 2909.
Nasa'i, as-Sunan, vol. 5, p. 216 # 2904.
Nasa'i, as-Sunan al-kubra, vol. 2, p. 392 # 3887 & vol. 6, p. 337 # 11152.
Ahmad bin Hambal, al-Musnad, vol. 2, p. 220 # 7053.

up into the heavens before the coming of *Qiyamah* so that neither of them experience the events of *Qiyamah*.

Evidence will now be given from the Holy Qur'an and traditions to prove that these two places have eternal existence and can never face destruction, thus supporting the sayings of the *awliya*.

The Rawda of the Prophet ﷺ and the surrounding part of Madinah will also be raised to the heavens. Since the Prophet ﷺ is an embodiment of existence, there can never be 'an end' there. The earth where the Rawda of the Prophet ﷺ is situated is not from this planet. It is a piece of Paradise. The holy grave of the Prophet ﷺ is also in this area and His ﷺ grave is not even from the soil of this world.

> *'The ground between my Minbar and my house is a meadow from the Gardens of Paradise'*

This hadith mentioned above, is still displayed on the entrance into *Riyadu'l-Jannah*. It has not been removed by the present Saudi government. If this tradition cannot be erased from the entrance, then surely the Rawda itself cannot be demolished.

The Holy Quran also cannot perish; it too will be raised to the heavens from both books and hearts.

عَنْ عَبْدِ اللهِ بنِ عَمْرٍو: لَا تَقُومُ السَّاعَةُ حَتَّى يَرجِعَ الْقُرآنُ مِنْ حَيْثُ جَاءَ، فَيَكُونُ لَهُ دَوِيٌّ حَوْلَ الْعَرْشِ كَدَوِيِّ النَّحْلِ. فَيَقُولُ لَهُ الرَّبُّ: مَا لَكَ؟ فَيَقُولُ: مِنكَ خَرَجْتُ وَإِلَيكَ أَعُودُ أُتْلَى، وَلَا يُعْمَلُ بِي، فَعِنْدَ ذَلِكَ يُرْفَعُ الْقُرآنُ.

Abdullah bin ʿAmr narrates: the hour will never happen until the Quran returns to where it has come from. It will have humming like the humming of the bee around the throne of Allah (it will complain to the Lord Almighty about something and that will be heard around the ʿArsh of Allah). The Lord will say, 'What is the matter? (What do you have to say?)'. it will say, 'from you I went out and towards you I return in a state that I am read/recited (only) and not practiced. At that time, the Quran will be raised.[4]

Hearts and paper can perish whereas the Holy Quran is eternal. People will wake up in the morning, open copies of the Holy Quran and find that the pages are blank. So the Holy Quran, the Rawda of the Prophet ﷺ and the Kaʿbah will be raised to the heavens.

Allah says in the Qur'an:

[4] Daylami, al-Firdaws, vol. 5, p. 79, # 7513

خَالِدِينَ فِيهَا أَبَدًا لَّهُمْ فِيهَا أَزْوَاجٌ مُّطَهَّرَةٌ وَنُدْخِلُهُمْ ظِلًّا ظَلِيلًا

"they will remain in it (Jannah) Forever"

The seventh sign is *da'ba-tul-ard;* a huge beast.

عَنْ أَبِي هُرَيْرَةَ أَنَّ رَسُولَ اللَّهِ صَلَّى اللهُ عَلَيْهِ وَسَلَّمَ قَالَ: تَخْرُجُ الدَّابَّةُ مَعَهَا خَاتَمُ سُلَيْمَانَ وَعَصَا مُوسَى، فَتَجْلُو وَجْهَ الْمُؤْمِنِ وَتَخْتِمُ أَنْفَ الْكَافِرِ بِالْخَاتَمِ حَتَّى إِنَّ أَهْلَ الْخِوَانِ لَيَجْتَمِعُونَ، فَيَقُولُ: هَاهَا يَا مُؤْمِنُ. وَيُقَالُ: هَاهَا يَا كَافِرُ. وَيَقُولُ هَذَا: يَا مُؤْمِنُ. وَيَقُولُ هَذَا: يَا كَافِرُ.

"Abu Hurayrah states that the Messenger of Allah ﷺ said, "The beast will appear (near the Last Hour) possessing the ring of Sulaiman and Musa's stick. It would enlighten the believer's face and seal the nose of the disbeliever with the (seal on the) ring until the people of (dining) tray assemble (it could refer to the people of worldly interests only or the non believers). So this (man) would say, "Ha ha, O believer" and it will be said, "Ha ha, O infidel." And this will say: O believer.' And this (other one) will say: O infidel.'[5]

---

[5] Tirmidhi graded it hasan (fair) in as-Sunan, vol. 5, p. 340 # 3187.
Ibn Majah, as-Sunan, vol. 2, p. 1351, # 4066.
Ahman bin Hambal, al-Musnad, vol. 2, pp. 295, 491 # 7924, 10366.
Hakim, al-Mustadrak, vol. 4, p. 532 # 8494.
Nu'aym bin Hammad, Kitab-ul-fitn, vol. 2, p. 665 # 1861.

The eighth sign is that a breeze bearing a pleasant scent will emanate from Yemen and all believers will pass away upon inhaling it. The Holy Prophet ﷺ said that the torture of Qiyamah will not take place on any believer. This is the great level of respect that exists for *awliya*, *sulaha* and pious people. They are preserved from experiencing the earthquakes and calamities of *Qiyamah*. Only *kafirs*, hypocrites and evil people will be alive at that time to experience the calamities.

عَنْ عَائِشَةَ قَالَتْ: سَمِعْتُ رَسُولَ اللَّهِ صَلَّى اللهُ عَلَيْهِ وَآلِهِ وَسَلَّمَ يَقُولُ: لَا يَذْهَبُ اللَّيْلُ وَالنَّهَارُ حَتَّى تُعْبَدَ اللَّاتُ وَالْعُزَّى. فَقُلْتُ: يَا رَسُولَ اللَّهِ! إِنْ كُنْتُ لَأَظُنُّ حِينَ أَنْزَلَ اللَّهُ: هُوَ الَّذِي أَرْسَلَ رَسُولَهُ بِالْهُدَى وَدِينِ الْحَقِّ لِيُظْهِرَهُ عَلَى الدِّينِ كُلِّهِ وَلَوْ كَرِهَ الْمُشْرِكُونَ. أَنَّ ذَلِكَ تَامًّا. قَالَ: إِنَّهُ سَيَكُونُ مِنْ ذَلِكَ مَا شَاءَ اللَّهُ، ثُمَّ يَبْعَثُ اللَّهُ رِيحًا طَيِّبَةً فَتَوَفَّى كُلَّ مَنْ فِي قَلْبِهِ مِثْقَالُ حَبَّةِ خَرْدَلٍ مِنْ إِيمَانٍ. فَيَبْقَى مَنْ لَا خَيْرَ فِيهِ، فَيَرْجِعُونَ إِلَى دِينِ آبَائِهِمْ.

"'Aisha ﷺ states, "I heard the Prophet ﷺ say, 'Day and night will not pass away (time will not finish or the day of judgment will not come) until people begin to worship Lat and 'Uzza' (two goddesses of pre-Islamic Arabia). I said, 'O Messenger of Allah, when Allah revealed the Ayah "It is He Who has sent His Apostle with Guidance and the Religion of Truth, to proclaim over all religion, even though the Pagans may detest (it)" (al-Tawbah 9:33), I

> *thought this was a complete (dominance of the truth and none will ever worship those idols)'. The Prophet ﷺ said, 'whatever Allah wills out of that will happen (meaning that He only knows the real meaning and the extent of its application - i.e. how long this state will stay undisturbed). Then Allah will send a pleasant breeze, which will take everyone who has as much faith as a grain of mustard-seed in his heart. Only those with no goodness in them will be left, and they will revert to the religion of their forefathers'"*[6]

After all the believers have passed away there will be a period of one hundred and twenty years. In that period the whole world will consist of *kafirs*, sinners, oppressors, liars and adulterers.

There is a tradition that the Prophet ﷺ said that in those one hundred and twenty years the Arabs would again worship the same idols.

The ninth sign is the rising of the sun from the West. After a long night the sun will rise from the West and after midday it will set again.

---

[6] Muslim, as-Sahih, vol. 4, p. 2230, # 2907.
Muqri, as-Sunan al-warida fi al-fitn, vol. 4, p. 830 # 426.
Bayhaqi, as-Sunan al-kubra, vol. 9, p. 181 # 18401.

عَنْ أَبِي هُرَيْرَةَ رَضِيَ اللّٰهُ عَنْهُ، قَالَ: قَالَ رَسُولُ اللّٰهِ صَلَّى اللّٰهُ عَلَيْهِ وَآلِهِ وَسَلَّمَ: لَا تَقُومُ السَّاعَةُ حَتَّى تَطْلُعَ الشَّمْسُ مِنْ مَغْرِبِهَا، فَإِذَا رَآهَا النَّاسُ آمَنَ مَنْ عَلَيْهَا، فَذَاكَ حِينَ لَا يَنْفَعُ نَفْسًا إِيمَانُهَا، لَمْ تَكُنْ آمَنَتْ مِنْ قَبْلُ.

"Abu Hurayrah states that the Messenger of Allah ﷺ said, "The Hour will not be established until the sun rises from the West and when the people see it they will have faith. But that will be (the time) when believing of the soul, that will have not believed before that time, will not benefit it."[7]

The final signs will be *nafkhatu'l-ula* when the trumpet will be blown for the first time. The first calamitous noise will be heard and will result in all the people dying. It is also known as *nafkhatu'l-imatah.* There will then be a further period of forty years, after which the trumpet will be blown for the second time.

At the second blow everyone will come back to life and this will be *ba'as ba'da'l-mawt*, *Qiyamah* will have taken place. Everyone will be naked and running towards the Place of Gathering. The enemies of Allah ﷻ will be travelling on their faces with their legs upright. Others will be on foot, whereas some people will be

[7] Agreed upon by Bukhari and Muslim.
Bukhari, as-Sahih, vol. 4, p. 1697, # 4359.
Muslim, as-Sahih, vol. 1, p. 137 # 157.
Tirmidhi, as-Sunan, vol. 5, p. 264 # 3072.
Abu Dawud, as-Sunan, vol. 4, p. 115 # 4312.
Ibn Maja, as-Sunan, vol. 2, pp. 1352, 1353 # 4068, 4070.
Nasa'i, as-Sunan al-kubra, vol. 6, p. 343 # 11177.

provided with horses and others with camels. Prophet ﷺ said that he will provide his she-camel for his daughter Sayyidah Fatimah رضي الله عنها and He ﷺ will be travelling on *buraq* accompanied by seventy thousand angels.

The length of time between Imam Mahdi's appearance and Qiyamah

The events have been mentioned in the sequence in which they will take place immediately after the appearance of Imam Muhammad Mahdi عليه السلام. So those who have announced that Imam Muhammad Mahdi عليه السلام is here and is shortly to announce his arrival, should realise that this is not a minor claim to make. When it is said that Imam Muhammad Mahdi عليه السلام is here, it also means that Qiyamah is not far behind.

Imam Muhammad Mahdi عليه السلام will live for a further forty years after his appearance. His *khulafa*, al-Mansur and al-Mahdi, will rule for twenty-three or twenty seven years after him.

The Prophet ﷺ said that the pleasant smelling breeze will come at the start of the century due to which all believers will pass away. The sun will rise from the West at that time. After that there will be a period of one hundred and twenty years exclusively for the kuffar, this period will be followed by the first blow of the trumpet.

All of these events are mentioned in traditions that have been quoted from *Sihah Sittah* and other collections.

There will be a period of forty years between the first and

second blasts of the trumpet. During that period there will be *dukhan* (smoke), which will last for forty days and a fire will take place. On the second blow of the trumpet people will rise after death and the Gathering will take place.

The duration of each period in terms of years has been given, as mentioned in *Sahih* traditions. Moreover the coming of Imam Mahdi is not disconnected with the coming of Qiyamah, they are both linked and will occur with a short period between them.

After the passing away of Imam Muhammad Mahdi ﵇, *Qiyamah* will take place after a maximum of two hundred to three hundred years.

The true knowledge of when Qiyamah will take place is with Allah ﷻ:

يَسْأَلُونَكَ عَنِ السَّاعَةِ أَيَّانَ مُرْسَاهَا قُلْ إِنَّمَا عِلْمُهَا عِندَ رَبِّي لَا يُجَلِّيهَا
لِوَقْتِهَا إِلَّا هُوَ ثَقُلَتْ فِي السَّمَاوَاتِ وَالْأَرْضِ لَا تَأْتِيكُمْ إِلَّا بَغْتَةً يَسْأَلُونَكَ
كَأَنَّكَ حَفِيٌّ عَنْهَا قُلْ إِنَّمَا عِلْمُهَا عِندَ اللَّهِ وَلَٰكِنَّ أَكْثَرَ النَّاسِ لَا يَعْلَمُونَ ○

They ask thee of the (destined) Hour, when will it come to port. Say: Knowledge thereof is with my Lord only. He alone will manifest it at its proper time. It is heavy in the heavens and the earth. It cometh not to you save unawares. They question thee as if thou couldst be well informed thereof. Say: Knowledge thereof is with Allah only, but most of mankind know not. [8]

Nevertheless, we can assess from the twelve signs given in traditions that the length of time between Imam Muhammad Mahdi عليه السلام and *Qiyamah* will be two to three hundred years. Therefore to proclaim that Imam Mahdi عليه السلام has appeared is ludicrous as it is also a proclamation of Qiyamah.

[8] Qur'an (al-Araf'), 7: 187

CHAPTER TEN

THE APPEARANCE OF IMAM MAHDI عليه السلام

Absolute knowledge of the appearance of Imam Mahdi ﷺ is possessed only by Allah ﷻ, as it is knowledge of the Unseen, and He ﷻ when He wills, gives this knowledge to His Messengers. The Prophet ﷺ did not reveal exact details but he did reveal the Signs of the coming of Qiyamah. So only Allah ﷻ and His Prophet ﷺ have correct knowledge of that.

The exact year of the coming of Imam Muhammad Mahdi ﷺ has, however, been calculated by examining the dates that are mentioned in the traditions of the Prophet ﷺ.

By collating all this information, one can approximate the year in which Imam Mahdi ﷺ will appear. The research has been carried out only through the blessing of the Prophet ﷺ. If the calculation is correct then the traditions of the Prophet ﷺ have been understood.

If it is wrong then it is due to the deficiency of the research and incorrect understanding. In any case what the Prophet ﷺ said, is of course, absolutely true.

No man can give the exact date and time of the coming of Imam Mahdi ﷺ with certainty. We can only make a calculation on the basis of the evidence in our possession. The reason why it is so vital to announce the year of the birth of Imam Muhammad Mahdi ﷺ is because of the increased speculation about it and the continual announcements being made by people, that Imam

Muhammad Mahdi ﷺ has appeared. His arrival into this world will be a momentous event bringing with it the final era of mankind on earth, fulfilling Allah's promise of the end and concluding humanity.

It must be stressed again that he will be the last caliph and imam of the Holy Prophet's ﷺ *ummah.* The Holy Prophet ﷺ was proud of him and mentioned him and his time in great detail.

After studying many traditions, with the help of Allah ﷻ and blessings of the Prophet ﷺ, the year of the appearance of Imam Muhammad Mahdi ﷺ has been calculated.

عَنْ أَبِي قَتَادَةَ قَالَ: قَالَ رَسُولُ اللهِ صَلَّى اللهُ عَلَيْهِ وَآلِهِ وَسَلَّمَ: اَلْآيَاتُ بَعْدَ الْمِائَتَيْنِ.

Abu Qatadah reported that Allah's Messenger ﷺ said, "The signs (will appear) after year 200."[1]

In *Sunan Ibn Majah, Kitabu'l-fitan, Babu'l-ayaat*, hadith no. 4057, the twelve signs are mentioned extensively up to the people waking up and going from their graves to the "Place of Gathering". Following that there is a hadith narrated by Anas bin Malik ﷺ from Abu Qatadah ﷺ that the Prophet ﷺ said that the signs will

[1] Ibn Majah, as-Sunan, vol. 2, p. 1348, # 4057.
Hakim graded it sahih (sound) according to the conditions of Bukhari and Muslim in al-Mustadrak, vol. 4, p. 475 # 8319.
Daylami, Musnad al-firdaws, vol. 1, p. 125 # 434.

take place after the completion of a second century of the Hijrah calendar. In other words after the second century of a particular millennium. Of course, the first of those signs is the coming of Imam Muhammad Mahdi ﷺ. At present we are in the fifth century of the second millennium of the al-Hijrah calendar.

All the signs and events mentioned were compiled by Imam at-Tabrizi in *Mishkat al-Masabih, Kitabu'l-fitan, Bab ashrat as-sa'ah* (Signs preceding the Last Hour). In the third section there is a hadith that states that the signs will appear after the second century (of a particular millennium).

Al-Mustadrak of Imam al-Hakim states in hadith no. 8319 that the signs will start in the second century of the Hijra. Imam al-Hakim has said that this tradition is *sahih* according to the conditions of Imams al-Bukhari and Muslim. Imam Jalalu'd-din as-Suyuti related it in *al-Hawi lil-Fatawa* and other *muhaditheen* have also related it. Imam Nu'aym ibn Hammad, the shaykh of Imam al-Bukhari, has it in his *Kitabu'l-fitan*. All these imams and *muhaditheen* relayed, through different chains of transmission, that these signs will take place in the second century after the completion of a thousand years.

Bearing in mind the overriding principle that the statement of the Prophet ﷺ supersedes and overrules any calculation made by anyone, the Holy Prophet ﷺ has indeed specified the date of the appearance of Imam Mahdi ﷺ and the details have come in the books of *sihah sittah*. We are now in the year 1428 AH and in the fifth century of this particular millennium of the Hijra.

The Prophet ﷺ said that the twelve signs of *Qiyamah* would start in the second century of a post Hijra millennium and we are now in the fifth century. If Imam Muhammad Mahdi عليه السلام were to have come in this millennium, then the time for his appearance has already passed, by about two hundred years. He should have appeared after 1200 AH. If he had appeared 225 years ago then today we would have been involved in the process of accounting for our actions in the Place of Gathering. The reason for that being, as mentioned earlier through traditions, that after the passing away of Imam Muhammad Mahdi عليه السلام the twelve signs and *Qiyamah* will take place within two to three hundred years.

So it is clear that Imam Muhammad Mahdi عليه السلام cannot appear in the present millennium. So those who want to announce his appearance cannot do so this millennium. This is according to the words of the Holy Prophet ﷺ. The earliest that Imam Muhammad Mahdi عليه السلام can now appear is after the completion of the second century of the next millennium. That is after a minimum of seven hundred and seventy five years from now.

The new century will start in about seven hundred and seventy five years time, that is if the next millennium is considered to be the correct millennium. If we do not accept the next millennium to be the correct one for the appearance of Imam Muhammad Mahdi عليه السلام, then it will have to be at least another thousand years later. One thing that the Prophet ﷺ made categorically clear, something that cannot change in the slightest, is that although the correct millennium may be one or another, the century cannot change and Imam Mahdi عليه السلام will certainly appear after the completion of two centuries of the millennium concerned. The Holy Prophet ﷺ pinpointed the completion of the second century after a millennium, for the beginning of the signs and as we know, the first of those signs is the appearance of Imam Muhammad Mahdi ﷺ.

No one can determine the correct millennium. Many changes will take place in that time. There is a clear possibility of all of the necessary changes in world affairs mentioned earlier taking place within the next eight hundred years, if indeed the next millennium is the correct one.

عَنْ أَبِي قَبِيلٍ، قَالَ: اجْتِمَاعُ النَّاسِ عَلَى الْمَهْدِي سَنَةَ أَرْبَعٍ وَمِائَتَيْنِ.

"Abu Qabeel ﷺ states, "The people will assemble with Imam Mahdi in the year 204."[2]

Imam Nu'aym ibn Hammad, the shaykh of Imams al-Bukhari, Muslim, at-Tirmidhi and others relates in *Kitabu'l-Fitan* a hadith, which was quoted by Imam Jalalu'd-din as-Suyuti in *al-Hawi lil-Fatwah* and also by other imams, which says that Imam Muhammad Mahdi ﷺ will appear and there will be *ba'yah* at his hand, and the year of his appearance will be the fourth year. As we know that it will be in the third century, so the appearance of Imam Muhammad Mahdi ﷺ, and the *ba'yah* that will be taken at

[2] Nu'aym bin Hammad, Kitab-ul-Fitan, vol. 1, p. 334, # 962.

his hand, will take place in the year 204.

If we consider that the next millennium is the correct one and that all the aforementioned events can take place in the natural course of things before that time, then the earliest chance for the appearance of Imam Muhammad Mahdi عليه السلام is in the year 2204 AH. It is now 1428 AH, so the minimum amount of time, which must elapse before his appearance, is seven hundred and seventy-six years. That is only if the next millennium is the millennium of the appearance of Imam Muhammad Mahdi عليه السلام and the Signs of *Qiyamah*. If it is not then it may be the millennium after that. It may be any millennium but the year 204 is certain.

So before scholars talk of the appearance of Imam Muhammad Mahdi عليه السلام they should first look at which century they are in. As the signs of the coming of Imam Mahdi عليه السلام and Prophet Isa عليه السلام will begin after the completion of two centuries into the millennium, that time has already passed in the present one. So the earliest when Imam Muhammad Mahdi عليه السلام can appear is the year 2204 AH which is equivalent to 2783 CE.

Wallahu a'lam bissawab

If I am wrong then I seek forgiveness from Allah سبحانه وتعالى. If what I have said is true then it is true because the saying of the Holy Prophet Muhammad ﷺ is true and *haqq*.

Shaykh-ul-Islam Dr. Muhammad Tahir-ul-Qadri

BIBLIOGRAPHY

1. *The Holy Qur'an*, Revealed by Almighty Allah
2. 'Abd-ur-Razzaq, Abu bakr, San'ani (126-211/744-826), *al-Musannaf*, Karachi, Pakistan: al-Majlis-ul-'ilmi, 1st ed. 1390/1970.
3. Abu Dawud, Sulayman bin Ash'ath (202-275/817-889), *as-Sunan*, Beirut, Lebanon: Dar Ihya'-it-turath-il-'arabi, n.d.
4. Abu Nu'aym, Ahmad bin 'Abdullah Asbahani (336-430/948-1038), *Hilyat-ul-awliya' wa tabaqat-ul-asfiya'*, Beirut, Lebanon: Dar-ul-kitab-il-'arabi, 3rd ed. 1400/1980.
5. Abu Ya'la, Ahmad bin 'Ali (210-307/825-919), *al-Musnad*, Damascus, Syria: Dar-ul-ma'mun lit-turath, 1st ed. 1404/1984.
6. Ahmad bin Hambal, Ibn Muhammad (164-241/780-855), *al-Musnad*, Beirut, Lebanon: al-Maktab-ul-Islami, 2nd ed. 1398/1978.
7. Bayhaqi, Ahmad bin Husayn (384-458/994-1066), *as-Sunan-ul-kubra*, Multan, Pakistan: Nashr-us-sunnah, n.d.
8. Bazzar, Abu Bakr Ahmad bin 'Amr (210-292/825-905), *al-Musnad*, Beirut, Lebanon: Mu'assissa 'ulum-il-Qur'an, 1st ed. 1409 AH.
9. Bukhari, Muhammad bin Isma'il (194-256/810-870), *as-Sahih*, Damascus, Syria: Dar-ul-qalam, 1st ed. 1401/1981.
10. Bukhari, Muhammad bin Isma'il (194-256/810-870), *at-Tarikh-ul-kabir*, Beirut, Lebanon: Dar-ul-kutub-il-'ilmiyyah, n.d.
11. Daylami, Abu Shuja' Shirawayh (445-509/1053-1115), *al-Firdaws*, Beirut, Lebanon: Dar-ul-kutub-il-'ilmiyyah, 1st ed. 1986.
12. Hakim, Abu 'Abdullah Muhammad ibn 'Abdullah (321-405/933-1014), *al-Mustadrak*, Beirut, Lebanon: Dar-ul-kutub-il-'ilmiyyah, 1st ed. 1411/1990.

13. Haythami, 'Ali bin Abu Bakr (735-807/1335-1405), *Majma'-uz-zawa'id*, Cairo, Egypt: Dar-ur-riyan lit-turath, 1407/1987.
14. Hindi, 'Ala'-ud-Din 'Ali (d.975ah), *Kanz-ul-'ummal*, Beirut, Lebanon: Mu'assisat-ur-risalah, 2nd ed. 1407/1986.
15. Ibn 'Abd-ul-Barr, Yusuf bin 'Abdullah (368-463/979-1071), *al-Istidhkar*, Beirut, Lebanon: Dar-ul-kutub-il-'ilmiyyah, 1st ed. 2000 AD.
16. Ibn Abi 'Asim, Ahmad bin Amr Shaybani (206-287 AH), *Kitab-ul-Jihad*, Medina, Saudi Arab: Maktaba al-ulum wa al-hikam, 1st ed, 1409.
17. Ibn Abi Shaybah, Abu Bakr 'Abdullah bin Muhammad (159-235/776-850), *al-Musannaf*, Riyadh, Saudi Arab: Maktaba ar-Rushd, 1st ed. 1409 AH.
18. Ibn 'Adi, Abu Ahmad 'Abdullah (277-365/890-976), *al-Kamil*, Beirut, Lebanon: Dar-ul-fikr, 3rd ed. 1409/1988.
19. Ibn 'Asakir, Abu al-Qasim 'Ali bin Hasan (499-571/1105-1176), *Tarikh Dimash al-Kabir*, generally known as *Tarikh Ibn 'Asakir*, Beirut, Lebanon: Dar al-fikr, 2001 AD.
20. Ibn Ishaq, Muhammad (360-395 AH), *Min hadith Khaythama*, Cairo, Egypt: Maktaba al-Qur'an, n.d.
21. Ibn Majah, Muhammad bin Yazid (209-273/824-887), *as-Sunan*, Beirut, Lebanon: Dar Ihya'-it-turath-il-'arabi, 1395/1975.
22. Ibn Mansur, Khurasani (d. 277 AH), India: Dar as-salf, 1st ed. 1403/1982.
23. Muqri, Abu 'Amr 'Uthman bin Sa'id (371-444 AH), *as-Sunan al-warida fi al-fitn*, Riyadh, Saudi Arab: Dar al-'Asima, 1st ed. 1416 AH.

24. Muslim, Ibn-ul-Hajjaj Qushayri (206-261/821-875), *as-Sahih*, Beirut, Lebanon: Dar Ihya'-it-turath-il-'arabi, n.d.

25. Nasa'i, Ahmad bin Shu'ayb (215-303/830-915), *as-Sunan al-kubra*, Beirut, Lebanon: Dar-ul-kutub-il-'ilmiyyah, 1st ed. 1411/1991.

26. Nasa'i, Ahmad bin Shu'ayb (215-303/830-915), *as-Sunan*, Beirut, Lebanon: Dar-ul-kutub-il-'ilmiyyah, n.d.

27. Ibn Hammad, Abu 'Abdullah Nu'aym (d. 229/884), *Kitab-ul-fitan*, Cairo, Egypt: Maktabat-ut-tawhid, 1st ed. 1412.

28. Qazwini, Abd al-Karim bin Muhammad, *at-Tadwin fi akhbar Qazwin*, Beirut, Lebanon: Dar-ul-kutub-il-'ilmiyyah, 1987 AD.

29. Qurtubi, Abu 'Abdullah, Muhammad bin Ahmad (284-380/897-990), *al-Jami' li-ahkam-il-Qur'an*, Beirut, Lebanon: Dar Ihya'-it-turath-il-'arabi, 2nd ed., n.d.

30. Shawkani, Muhammad bin 'Ali bin Muhammad (1173-1250/1760-1834), *Fath-ul-qadir*, Egypt: 1383 AH.

31. Suyuti, Jalal-ud-Din 'Abd-ur-Rahman (849-911/1445-1505), *ad-Durr-ul-manthur*, Beirut, Lebanon: Dar al-Fikr, 1993 AD.

32. Suyuti, Jalal-ud-Din 'Abd-ur-Rahman (849-911/1445-1505), *al-Hawi lil-fatawa*, Beirut, Lebanon: Dar-ul-kitab-il-'arabi, 1425/2005.

33. Tabarani, Sulayman bin Ahmad (260-360/873-971), *al-Mu'jam-ul-awsat*, Riyadh, Saudi Arabia: Maktabat-ul-ma'arif, 1st ed. 1405/1985.

34. Tabarani, Sulayman bin Ahmad (260-360/873-971), *al-Mu'jam-ul-kabir*, Cairo, Egypt: Maktabah Ibn Taymiyyah, n.d.

35. Tabarani, Sulayman bin Ahmad (260-360/873-971), *al-Mu'jam-ul-kabir*, Mosul, Iraq: Matba't-uz-zuhra'-il-hadithah, 2nd ed., n.d.

36. Ibn Jarir Tabari, Abu Ja'far Muhammad (224-310/839-923), *Jami'-ul-bayan fi tafsir-il-Qur'an*, Beirut, Lebanon: Dar-ul-ma'rifah, 4th ed. 1400/1980.

37. Tirmidhi, Muhammad bin 'Isa (210-279/825-892), *al-Jami'-us-sahih*, Beirut, Lebanon: Dar Ihya'-it-turath-il-'arabi, n.d.

NOTES

NOTES

NOTES

NOTES